D0037560

Past Masters
General Editor Keith Thomas

Chaucer

Past Masters

George Kane

Chaucer

Oxford   New York

OXFORD UNIVERSITY PRESS

1984

Oxford University Press, Walton Street, Oxford OX2 6DP

London New York Toronto
Delhi Bombay Calcutta Madras Karachi
Kuala Lumpur Singapore Hong Kong Tokyo
Nairobi Dar es Salaam Cape Town
Melbourne Auckland

and associated companies in
Beirut Berlin Ibadan Mexico City Nicosia

Oxford is a trade mark of Oxford University Press

British Library Cataloguing in Publication Data
Kane, George
Chaucer.—(Past masters)
1. Chaucer, Geoffrey—Criticism and
interpretation
I. Title II. Series
821'.1 PR1924
ISBN 0–19–287596–5
ISBN 0–19–287595–7 Pbk

Library of Congress Cataloging in Publication Data
Kane, George.
Chaucer.
(Past masters)
Bibliography: p.
Includes index.
1. Chaucer, Geoffrey, d. 1400—Criticism and interpretation.
I. Title.
PR1924.K33 1984 821'.1 84-11230
ISBN 0–19–287596–5
ISBN 0–19–287595–7 (pbk.)

Set by Hope Services, Abingdon
Printed in Great Britain by
St. Edmundsbury Press Ltd
Bury St. Edmunds, Suffolk

Contents

Acknowledgements

I am under obligation to the authors of most of the innumerable books and essays about Chaucer I have read, for teaching me or for making me think critically, but in particular to Talbot Donaldson, who first made the distinction between the speaking voice of Chaucer's poetry and its poet, and to the scholars who collected and edited the information in the *Chaucer Life Records* (see p. 119). My quotations are taken from F. N. Robinson's *The Works of Geoffrey Chaucer* (2nd edn., Oxford University Press, 1957), to which reference is by page number.

1 One man in his time

It took nearly a thousand years for the Europe that grew out of the barbarian invasions of the Roman Empire to bring forth poets to match those of classical antiquity: first Dante, and then, a couple of generations later, Langland and Chaucer. Of the three, Dante and Langland can appear easier to explain historically. Dante's *Divine Comedy* expressed that last moment when the intellectual centre of Europe was still the University of Paris, before the ecclesiastical establishment there banned theological speculation, and it still seemed possible to harmonize Neoplatonic transcendentalism and Thomas Aquinas's intensely cerebral Christianization of Aristotle. Langland, two generations after Dante, records the other side of the picture, the fears and unease, apocalyptic anxieties and perplexities of the late medieval Christian. By contrast the poetry of Chaucer, only a few years younger than Langland, answers to no comparatively facile characterization.

His relation to his times is in every respect complex. About his achievement there has seldom been any question. He was a legend almost from the moment of his death in 1400. Successive generations refashioned that legend in their own terms: he was the notable rhetorician, the 'father' of English poetry, the quaint Gothic humorist and, in more recent times, the urbanely or ironically witty genial sceptic, as good as modern. The sum and actuality of his achievement, as an Englishman writing in English in the later fourteenth century—itself a remarkable circumstance—is vastly more notable than

I

the legends suggest. And the explanation of how his work could present him and itself to successive generations in so many appearances is to be found in his personal circumstances and the time and place in which he wrote.

By the quality of his use of the English language, socially and culturally devalued since the Norman Conquest, Chaucer re-established its standing as a literary medium. In his earliest surviving work he successfully naturalized the prevailing contemporary French poetic mode. By the time of writing his next long poem he had outgrown his original French models and was fired with a new conception of the potential depth of poetry, and of its function. As his learning and intellectual cultivation advanced he emerged as the first 'man of letters' in Europe outside Italy. The culture of medieval France, that had so long dominated Europe, never produced one of his quality. Moreover he carried his learning without pomposity, sometimes with engagingly self-disparaging irony. His poetry enhanced the musicality of English verse and gave it new metres. It displayed the English language in all registers from the coarsest to the sublime. Its depth of learned reference and conceptual range are huge. It expressed the sustained operation of a superior intelligence both sympathetic and penetrating. It had phenomenal capacity to engage and to move. The sheer amount of it and its consistently high quality were formidable in combination. It showed that major literary achievement of unquestioned excellence was attainable by a poet writing in English. By that demonstration it came for subsequent English poets to represent, and thus established, an English literary tradition.

Without appreciable models and with only the most

jejune critical theories to guide him, Chaucer achieved an understanding of dramatic narrative that enabled him to realize, unmistakably, both tragedy and comedy in his stories. The personages in those stories, created with phenomenal insight into the underlying motives of human action and their expression as behaviour, are the founder-members of the gallery of literary figures that is one chief treasure of English culture. Their loving and understanding representation constitutes a poetic which Chaucer devised, where, by depth of reference and multiplicity of implication, he brought considerations of art and morality into the best accommodation possible in his world and time.

Nevertheless Chaucer was not a professional poet. From his boyhood he was in the royal service where, presently, the records show him, not enjoying the sinecures by which a favoured court poet might be rewarded, but in offices of responsibility always arduous and even dangerous, some of which required skill and delicacy in negotiation, and others financial and administrative expertise. The vast reading that his works attest, with which he fed his avidly curious intellect, had for years to be a leisure activity. To a first career of royal servant and a second of scholar he added a third, of writer.

The three activities were not simply or evenly complementary. Given the low status and limited concept of the role of the vernacular poet when Chaucer began to write, that is before he enhanced and elevated them, it was his practice of poetry that was the anomalous activity. As it turned out, much of the immediate power of engagement of his poetry actually derives from this circumstance. For it prompted him to adopt, already in his earliest surviving work, and to develop and maintain

3

in almost all his writing, an authorial personality that must, from its nature, necessarily be fictitious. The speaking voice of his poetry, which by implication we are invited to identify as the author's, represents itself as imperceptive, even obtuse, lacking in sensibility. That fiction is one means by which Chaucer's poetry exercises engagement, but it is much more than a comic device: Chaucer developed it into an instrument of meaning that compels attention and thoughtfully evaluative response.

The England that Chaucer grew up and lived in was calculated to generate complex, potentially ambivalent attitudes in a mind of high intelligence disinclined to self-deception as Chaucer's evidently was. The fourteenth and fifteenth centuries have been called the 'waning of the Middle Ages'. More correctly there was never a typical 'medieval moment'. The whole period from the twelfth century on, when the European nations as we know or knew them had taken shape, was a time of change. What in the later Middle Ages has been seen as decay was actually accelerated change, with its concomitant disintegration. And in Chaucer's lifetime, of all Europe England was most affected by that condition, which was variously signalled.

Within months of Chaucer's birth in late 1345 or early 1346, the defeat of the glorious chivalry of France at the battle of Crécy through effective use of the longbow as an armour-piercing weapon ended the primacy of massed charges by mailed cavalry in warfare. An immediate consequence, which may actually have contributed to Chaucer's decision to write in English, was enhancement of the sense of national identity. A more remote one will have been the redistribution of power in Europe, by which England acquired a larger role: of this Chaucer's travels abroad on royal missions, and so to some degree his education and thus his poetic career, were a con- sequence.

Radical social changes took effect in his lifetime. One was economic: the final replacement of the old, self-sufficient manorial economy by a mercantile one. Improved agricultural methods made possible farming for the market, beyond the needs of manor or castle granary. Goods could be safely moved to trade centres. Money could be transferred by document across Europe. Now a shrewd man could speculate in commodities or even in currency. In such ways England prospered. Where once the only material wealth had been land, and great landowners might live out their lives in a shortage of ready money, and if you were not born to land you could acquire it only by conferment in feudal tenancy as a reward for military prowess, now a skilled craftsman with a gift for management, or a clever trader, could become rich in money terms. That might come to seem an end in itself; or if there were enough money your daughter could marry land and standing. Money was power. In Chaucer's early and middle years, in the larger English cities a wealthy merchant class was discovering its power. Chaucer came from that class and as a royal officer had to work with its magnates. His later writing shows insight into the effect of wealth, or the drive for it or for what it buys, upon personality.

Another change was the disintegration of the servile system in which the peasant had been *adscriptus glebae*, legally bound to the land he worked for his feudal lord. The disintegration came about through shortage of labour caused by the Black Death. It has been estimated that after the third epidemic in 1369 the population was reduced from something like three million by about a half. With each epidemic it had become harder for landowners to farm their estates. Wages for all kinds of labour rose by a documented 60 per cent in the decade after 1348. Many villeins fled the land for the high pay to be got for even casual labour, and landowners were driven to lease in free tenancy, sometimes to fugitives from other estates, land formerly worked by their own serfs. It was the initially low population of England that made this situation acute, but the effect was that England was the first country in Europe where the servile system broke down. One likes to think that if Chaucer had perceived what was in process he would have applauded it. But he cannot have done so: the conceptual matrices for such perception had not yet taken shape. Nevertheless he will have experienced a sense of the instability of his world, of the decay of institutions, the collapse of arrangements and systems a man had been brought up to rely on.

Chaucer's sense of instability will have been heightened as, growing into maturity, he observed at the closest range the state of the realm. The records show him in the king's service by 1366. That was the year before the battle of Nájera, the last of the great English victories of the fourteenth century, after which, with political ineptitude to match his father's, the Black Prince 'lost the peace'. Already by 1371 Edward III's health and mind were failing, and the Black Prince was incurably ill. The next king would be the child Richard of Bordeaux, and the saying from Ecclesiastes, 'Woe unto the land where a boy is king!', was on men's lips. Power accumulated in the hands of the unscrupulous around the ageing Edward. For the rest of the century control of the government of the realm was the object of contention between power groups in changing alignments. The shape of these in Richard II's reign was to affect Chaucer personally.

There were the great lords, Edward's younger sons and grandsons. Then came the baronage, owners of huge estates and often ambitious. These tended mainly to be against Richard's court party. The Commons, not as in our time elected, but drawn from the smaller land-owners and wealthier burgesses, were conceived of as speaking for the whole people. Given a courageous Speaker they were a force to be reckoned with, and when, in 1386–8, their interests coincided with those of the Lords, the two estates in combination were able to force the king to accept administrative reforms, and to eliminate his favourites. The London capitalists, hugely wealthy merchants whose loans, made less with expect-ation of financial advantage than for intangible con-siderations such as the royal favour and the influence this carried in their own circles, financed the enterprises of State or merely the royal extravagance, were mainly of the king's party.

From 1386 to 1389 the king himself was in conflict with a group of magnates, some his young uncles or cousins, who were determined to eliminate the court party. When, at length, in 1389 he asserted his full majority and right to independent action it became apparent, first that his whole intent was revenge upon those magnates, and second that his mental balance was disturbed. Finally, in 1399, the powers of the land accepted the appalling need to rise against their sovereign and to effect, or anyway acquiesce in, his deposition.

Geoffrey Chaucer's personality was formed, and his intellect acquired its interests and preoccupations, and his sensibility was developed in that world, pregnant with social and religious change and growth. The fortunes of his own family, by its expression of genetic energy in upward social movement, instance such change.

His great-grandfather, presumably a free peasant or artisan, migrated from the tiny village of Dennington, two miles north of Framlingham in Suffolk, to Ipswich where the records call him Andrew le Taverner. His grandfather, Robert Malin le Chaucer, or simply Robert le Chaucer, appears from the appellative to have learned a manufacturing trade, either shoemaker or hosier—the French word 'chaucier' is ambiguous. This was the first step up; he in his turn migrated to London where he established himself as a burgess and a wholesale importer of wine. The poet's father John, also in the wine trade, augmented the family's already substantial means (they held on to the Ipswich property) by marrying Agnes de Copton, niece and ward of the Keeper of the Royal Mint, from whom she presently inherited considerable London properties. That the poet himself was in the royal service, as the records show his grandfather to have been, if only briefly, in 1305, represents another step up, socially if not financially. His son Thomas followed him in the royal service, and became a very considerable landholder in Oxfordshire, Buckinghamshire and Hampshire, married to a co-heiress in a baronial family. The poet's granddaughter was married a third time—that establishes her financial and social eligibility—to William de la Pole, Earl and presently Duke of Suffolk.

The rise of those successive generations suggests energy, enterprise and exceptional ability. The poet's grandfather Robert was called 'Malin', of which the kindest translation is 'astute'. There were exceptional women in the family. When the poet's father John was twelve years old his paternal aunt, Robert Malin's sister, organized his abduction by force from London to Ipswich, intending to marry him to her daughter and thus keep the Ipswich property in the Suffolk branch. The attempt failed; from the size of the fine she was assessed to pay, and paid, she was a very wealthy woman. John himself was not a quiet boy. In 1327 at the age of about fifteen he served as a mounted man at arms against the Scots in a unit raised with City of London money, official and private; in 1329, soldiering with the same men he took part in the Earl of Lancaster's unsuccessful rising against Isabella and Mortimer. He was outlawed for that; the records name him as a ringleader in a raid by the troop on the Suffolk manor of Isabella's supporter the Abbot of Bury. A royal letter of protection of 1338 shows him travelling overseas in the king's service; he was on the staff of Edward III's expedition to Flanders which opened the Hundred Years War. He too, by good management and a good marriage, enlarged the family fortune. For a time he was deputy in Southampton to the king's chief butler, with duties in the collection of customs. The records show him, from 1337 until his death in 1366, as a wealthy man, a city freeman of standing and respect.

There is a particular reason why the heredity and background implied in those five generations must be taken into account. In Geoffrey Chaucer's poetry, most of it narrative related in the first person, we hear a speaking voice that powerfully suggests a narrator's personality. His readers over the centuries have variously constructed an actual poet from the tones they heard in that voice and the attitudes these suggested. Many of the constructs, however else they may differ, have in common two opposed notions, of an indisputably exceptional poet and a somehow ineffectual man. The idea of a poet embodying such a dichotomy is anachronistic, and typical of the Romantic period. It does not survive examination in the light of the history of Chaucer's family, where he is, so to speak, at the middle point, and of his own career in the royal service, where his standing was evidently high, for the offices he held were not sinecures conferred on an amusing and likeable entertainer, but positions demanding a man of ability, proven integrity and presence. It is altogether likely that some of the astuteness of grandfather Robert Malin entered into the creation of the suggested personality behind the speaking voice with its self-professed ineptitudes and preposterous value judgements.

Of the early formal education on which Chaucer's careers were based we have no personal records, but good general information. London merchant families like Chaucer's were literate in French and English; the men were highly numerate and often, for legal use, had learned some Latin. The women could read. In the London of his childhood there were three ecclesiastically authorized grammar schools, at least one of which had an excellent library, and numerous smaller, private schools. Boys were taught Latin grammar in French and thus learned French grammar as well. In one unidentified London school of the time they were taught English grammar. They were exposed to some rhetorical theory, contained in the standard Latin grammar. Their mathematical training was intense, mainly in computation, with a glance at astronomy. They read Latin poetry of the classical and later periods in a good anthology, *Liber Catonianus*. History and geography they picked up as they could. Much of their study was systematic memorizing, from which they acquired superbly retentive and productive memories.

The next stage of Chaucer's education is documented. Its character suggests that he had done well enough to be singled out, for by 1357 he was a member of the household and in the service of, first, Elizabeth Countess of Ulster, and then her husband Lionel, the king's second son. The records show him still in that service in 1360. Chaucer's introduction into a royal household can look like an adroit social manœuvre by his family, but more likely it reflects Edward III's policy of recruiting exceptional lay talent to outbalance the traditionally clerical element in his civil and political service. For this posts such as Chaucer's first one, in a royal household, were the training-ground. He will have entered Elizabeth's service as a page—the word means 'boy' in Middle English. In 1359, when he was about fourteen, he 'received arms', that is, became an esquire. He may even actually have soldiered (his father went to war at fourteen or fifteen), for he was a prisoner in French hands in March 1359. The king contributed a considerable sum towards his ransom. Whether blooded or not, he was already considered responsible: he carried dispatches from Calais to England for Lionel in October 1360. His standing as esquire must, however, be seen in historical terms. It does not mean that he had been touched with the mystique of romantic chivalry. His standing derived from the royal status of the man he served. The head cook and master carpenter in the household of Lionel's younger brother, John of Gaunt, were esquires. Service in a great household was a way to promotion; acceptable service earned it.

No records of Chaucer's life in the period 1361–5 have been found. Two of his more mature works reveal minute details of knowledge about Oxford and Cambridge that suggest the possibility of his having spent time at one or both universities. A sixteenth-century antiquarian wrote from hearsay of a record that would make Chaucer a student at the Inner Temple. It is certainly plausible that when young Chaucer's qualities of mind and personality had become evident, his royal employer, or even his father, arranged for his formal higher education. None of this, however, is verifiable.

At least part of the time he was abroad, in Aquitaine. In the royal archives of Navarre there is enrolled a copy of a safe-conduct, issued on 22 February 1365, for Geoffrey Chaucer, English esquire, three companions and their servants to move without let or hindrance throughout the kingdom until the coming feast of Pentecost. Chaucer was evidently in charge, and the winter journey implies urgency. Depending on whether the Navarrese recorder's year began at Christmas or on 25 March, Chaucer's mission had to do with attempts either to adjust the shifting Navarrese relation to the Anglo-Castilian alliance against Aragon, or to recall English mercenaries fighting on the enemy side. It looks as if, at this time, Chaucer was in the service of the Black Prince.

In and after 1367 the records show him as a 'king's esquire', a member of Edward's *familia*, the inner household which the king, in his prime, had formed and trained and liked best to use as an instrument of administration. In the summer of 1368 Chaucer was on assignment to an unspecified destination abroad, with a travel allowance that suggests a considerable journey. Between July and November of 1369 he was one of a number of king's esquires on campaign in France with the Duke of Lancaster, who had, presumably, asked for the loan of them as staff officers. In summer 1370 he was, in the terms of his warrant of protection, 'on the king's service overseas', probably to do with a treaty with Flanders. For six months of 1372–3 he was on a mission to Northern Italy with two Italians who stood high in Edward's service, specifically to negotiate a treaty port in England where merchant ships of the Genoese Republic could put in and discharge cargo without fear of seizure. This was a live issue: indeed, within months of Chaucer's return from this mission the king sent him to Dartmouth to effect release of a Genoese vessel under seizure by the local authorities. Meanwhile, from Genoa Chaucer went on alone to Florence 'on certain secret business of the king', very likely to negotiate a loan with the banking-house of Bardi. In 1376, along with Sir John Burley, he travelled 'on the king's secret business' to an unspecified destination, which, from the size of their expense allowances, was overseas. In 1377 Chaucer was abroad a number of times in France and Flanders, once at least in connection with a proposal of marriage between Richard, who that year succeeded to the throne, and a French princess. From May to September 1378 he was with Sir Edward Berkeley in Lombardy, treating with Barnabo Visconti, tyrant of Milan, and Sir John Hawkwood the English *condottiere* 'of certain needs touching the conduct of our war'. One last record of travel abroad shows him to have been at Calais with Sir William Beauchamp in the king's service in 1387.

These assignments, and many others within the realm, show Chaucer *in nuncio regis*, variously a king's messenger or an actual emissary. They clearly show that he must have been fluent in the dialects of northern and southern French and in Italian, and that those close to the king considered him of proven ability, discreet and dependable, a custodian of the royal interest both in negotiation with magnates and as the man behind a figurehead Sir This or That, who would take care of the subtleties of language and the detail of 'paperwork'. On 8 June 1374 he was appointed by royal warrant Controller of the Wool Custom and Wool Subsidy, and presently also of the less important Petty Custom.

The Wool Custom and Subsidy, a system of consolidated sales tax on wool, sheepskins and related commodities, levied at the point of export to ensure collection, was the main source of royal peacetime revenue. During Chaucer's controllership the annual total of revenue it produced was on average a quarter higher than that of the receipts from other sources as shown in the accounts of the royal wardrobe, the king's main financial agency. In Chaucer's time on average more than 1,000 consignments a year were handled in the Port of London. The tax for each had to be paid, after assignment, into the offices of two Collectors, appointed, like the Controller, by royal warrant. The Collectors were required to account in detail, consignment by consignment, for the accumulating revenue. The Controller's duty was to keep a 'counter-roll', a corresponding account against which, in the royal interest, the operations of the Collectors would be scrutinized. On taking office the Controller swore to ensure, to the best of his ability, that his lord the king would suffer no loss or damage whatever. Each licence to export, called a cocket, had to be authenticated by a seal of which the Controller held half the matrix, the Collectors the other. His terms of appointment expressly required the Controller to act in office in his own person, to write his accounts with his own hand, and to accept no gift in the execution of his duties.

The Controller was thus theoretically an auditor on

the king's behalf. There were circumstances which made Chaucer's particular situation in office formidable. The Collectors in his time were enormously wealthy City merchants to whom Edward, and then Richard, as often as not owed great sums. The two Collectors longest in office with Chaucer, Nicholas Brembre (1374–5 and 1377–87) and John Philipot (1377–83), were very close, aldermen together for many years, each in his turn Lord Mayor, both knighted for supporting Richard in the peasant rising of 1381, both members of the Grocers' Company, and brothers-in-law. Beyond that they were leaders of a small ring of merchants from the Grocers' and Fishmongers' Companies, which, from about 1365, had a virtual monopoly of the wool-export trade. In that year Brembre had shipped some 1,400 sacks. He was still among the most active traders in 1384–5, and in 1385–8 was Mayor of the Staple at Westminster.

Such was the situation Chaucer inherited. In the early days of the Custom the controllership had been designed as the key to its efficient administration. But Chaucer, late in the succession of royal servants in the post, was unlucky, both in the development of the London wool monopoly and in the extravagance of his two royal employers, each of whom repaid loans, whether from individuals, syndicates or the City of London itself, by assignment, that is charge, upon the receipts of the Wool Custom. Even had it been possible for one man to scrutinize operations on the scale of the collector-exporters', Chaucer would have been handicapped by his frequent mandated absences on other royal business, abroad or at home. There were even occasions when the royal debt to one or both Collectors was so huge that the Controller's half of the cocket seal was given as security.

By the 1370s, since Edward depended absolutely on such loans, the Controller's best service must necessarily have been to develop a relation between the parties in which the Collectors, who would use the proceeds of the Custom to repay themselves and their associates, would have always in mind that efficient and honest collection was in their own interest. The gains to them would be intangible as much as financial. A man who had begun as an apprentice would experience gratification from the sense of involvement in high policy. Like Richard Whittington half a generation later, who actually lost money as a financier of Henry V, they 'bought the royal ear and the royal eye', acquiring a say in the king's affairs, and thus valuable influence in their own world.

In that situation the Controller would still be a key man, notwithstanding his social and financial insignificance. For apart from the formal supervision that kept the mulcting of the royal revenue within the rules of the game, he would have to maintain good will between, on the one hand, an old man far into senility and then a pampered infantilist and, on the other, some of the most devious men in Europe. He himself would have to come to terms with that need to accommodate principle to expedience which is a morally debilitating feature of high finance, and his own integrity would necessarily be severely taxed. At the end of three years in office, on Edward's death in 1377, Chaucer's name was apparently good, for his commission was renewed. He remained Controller until he was replaced in December 1386: his tenure of office had been exceptionally long.

Chaucer's termination of office was unquestionably political, related to activities of the Parliament of late 1386, in which he himself sat as one of the two knights

of the shire for Kent. This was summoned for 1 October
to deliberate a threat of French invasion, but the danger
passed with the season, and Parliament turned its
attention inward. Lords and Commons united in demanding removal of the Chancellor and Treasurer, and
appointment of a 'great and continual council' to review
and amend the administration; this was to be, in effect, a
standing commission designed to abolish the power of
the group of men close to the king who, as they quite
correctly maintained, had taken advantage of his youth
and set him against his proper counsellors to the
detriment of the government of the realm. Among these
was Chaucer's long associate in the Custom and Subsidy,
Sir Nicholas Brembre. The king, at first defiant, gave in
to threats. By late autumn the commission had begun
sealing writs on its own account. Among these was one
appointing Chaucer's successor.

An express petition of the Commons had been for
dismissal of all Controllers in the ports of the realm
holding office for life. Chaucer, appointed at the king's
pleasure, might have been so regarded, but there is no
record that the petition was effective. More likely he
was singled out for a pair of connected reasons. First, he
was visible as one of five 'king's knights' in the
Commons: he had been arbitrarily appointed by the
Sheriff, whose return reads *elegi*, 'I have chosen'. Second,
he was a long associate of Brembre. That man was too
well entrenched to be touched as yet; it took two years
to bring him to face the charges of accroachment, that is,
usurpation of royal power, and of harmfully influencing
the king. Meanwhile he could be injured after a fashion
by attacking his associate.

Another possibility, that Chaucer asked to be relieved
of office, must be allowed. He may have offered himself

to Richard as a political sacrifice, or he may have had enough of the situation, or he may have sensed danger. In any event he did not leave in disgrace. He received the usual reimbursement for his sixty-one days service in Parliament. He submitted his final audit as Controller in due form. His annuities from the exchequer remained in effect. And he continued until July 1389 as a justice on the Commission of the Peace for Kent, to which he had been appointed in 1385.

In July 1389, two months after Richard asserted his majority, he appointed Chaucer his Clerk of the Works, the royal establishment with third or fourth charge upon the revenue. The office carried a heavy responsibility of accounting for building and maintenance. Chaucer's commission specifies the Palace of Westminster, the Tower, Berkhampstead Castle, royal manors at Byfleet, Chiltern Langley, Clarendon, Eltham, Feckenham, Kennington and Sheen, lodges in various royal forests, even a mews at Charing Cross. A year later the restoration of St George's (now the Prince Consort's) Chapel at Windsor was added to the list.

His staff included master-craftsmen designers and *purveyors*, local foremen, but he himself had to answer and account for innumerable details, from provision of materials and employment of workmen down to payment of gardeners' wages and itemizations of tools and machinery. There was a Controller to check his accounts. The post was dangerous: at least once Chaucer was attacked and robbed while carrying the king's money. The organization contained a potential of ill will, for the salaries of the Controller and the master-craftsmen were half that of the Clerk of the Works. Not many clerks continued in office long; Chaucer's term, just under two years, was about average. The clerkship was his last appointment in the royal service, though he continued a king's esquire for life.

Chaucer's career as a royal servant was neither grand nor undistinguished. Of the esquires named with him in Edward's household records of the 1360s, some married heiresses or widows of means and became landed, even titled gentlemen, and some disappeared from view. He belongs in a middle group, but there he stands out. Of his near contemporaries only two were as extensively employed *in nuncio regis*, Geoffrey Stukeley, whose last recorded mission was in 1376, and George Fellbridge, whose specialty was Flanders in the 1380s and 90s. Only one Controller between 1350 and 1400 held office longer than Chaucer, whose immediate successor was replaced after one year by a chamberlain of the exchequer, John Hermesthorpe, subsequently king's treasurer. Chaucer's predecessors in the clerkship had been the other chamberlain of the exchequer, Arnold Brocas, and Roger Elmham, the Clerk of the Privy Seal, men of evident standing.

In perspective he is to be seen not directing events but experiencing them very near the centre. He was unmistakably valued for his high intelligence, and given arduous, tedious or even dangerous offices of responsibility that called for skill and delicacy in negotiation as well as administrative and financial expertise. His duties always implied loyalty and trust.

His circumstances were comfortable enough. It is likely that his inheritance was substantial. The will of his father, who died in 1366, has not been found, but he was apparently the only son, and thus likely to have been principal beneficiary after reservation of a third of the estate for the widow, as was the custom in their class. From at least 1367 onward he had, as king's esquire, a regular income in the form of royal 'annuities', supplemented during his Controllership and Clerkship of the Works by remuneration of office as well as by occasional direct royal gifts or remissions of treasury loans. The rent-free lease of a house belonging to the City of London seems to have gone informally with the Controllership. By 1385 he owned property in the Greenwich area of Kent of sufficient value to make him liable for service on the Commission of the Peace for the county, and later as a Commissioner of Walls and Ditches.

He evidently had some of the astuteness of his grandfather, Robert Malin. Having been replaced in the Controllership in 1386, and observing the renewed purge of the royal household by the Merciless Parliament early in 1388, in May of that year he commuted his annuities by petitioning for their transfer to a man in a protected position. This was John Scalby, an esquire then on the staff of John Waltham who was Keeper of the Privy Seal in 1386, and one of the original commissioners that year appointed; he was to be rewarded with the see of Salisbury later in 1388. What consideration Chaucer received is not recorded, but the arrangment looks very much like a good turn done in dangerous times by one civil servant to another. Scalby, a shrewd Yorkshireman, was himself careful to have the annuities transferred, within three years, from the charge of the unsound exchequer to that of the County of Lincoln.

In 1394 Richard granted Chaucer a new exchequer annuity. We have no record that he held any formal royal appointment after the Clerkship of the Works. But in the papers of an eighteenth-century antiquary he is named with another as substitute or deputy forester of North Petherton in Somerset in 1390–1, and alone in 1397–8.

The nature and duties of that office are not clear. From 1386 to 1393 the hereditary keeper or forester, Roger Mortimer, Earl of March, then a minor, was involved in a suit in the Court of the Exchequer against the Crown's lessee of the forest. His guardians may, in 1390, have engaged Chaucer to safeguard his interest as accountant and auditor, or the Court of the Exchequer may have appointed Chaucer on his behalf. What the situation was in 1397–8 is quite obscure. In view of Chaucer's age and particular aptitudes, it seems improbable that he ever saw a tree in that 'forest'. But the association was apparently felicitous, for in 1405 Henry IV granted Chaucer's son Thomas lease of the forestership itself during the nonage of a new heir, Edmund Mortimer, who, on attaining his majority, leased the bailiwick of the forest to Thomas for life.

Chaucer seems to have enjoyed general regard in his last ten years. In 1395 Henry of Lancaster, then Earl of Derby, made him a present of a furred scarlet gown, and a further present of £10. That same year the king granted Chaucer a tun (210 imperial gallons) of wine annually. That genial conferment and Chaucer's annuities lapsed on Richard's deposition. But soon after his accession Henry reconferred them 'of his special grace and for good service'. Good service to two kings, and maybe also his poetry, were being acknowledged. In December 1399 Chaucer took the lease of a house in the garden of the Lady Chapel of Westminster Abbey, to be near the sound of bells in his old age, one likes to think. He died in 1400, on 25 October according to a sixteenth-century tradition.

2   Trial of strength

Chaucer's friend and contemporary John Gower wrote how Chaucer 'in the flower of his youth' had filled the country everywhere with poems and songs in praise of love, and Chaucer twice admits as much. But those early lyrics are lost or unidentifiable. The ones we have are mature, sometimes astringent writing. His earliest poem that we know of, *The Book of the Duchess*, is already a mature work. In one respect it is as predictable as was his youthful composition of love lyrics: it is written as from within the court, in the manner of French court poetry, and in that manner relates to a royal occasion. In all other particulars it is remarkable enough to presage Chaucer's later work.

The occasion was the death, in September 1368, of Blanche, Duchess of Lancaster, the wife of Edward's third living son, John of Gaunt or Ghent. The poem, a calculated replication in English of the most fashionable French poetic modes, is one of the most important events in the history of English literature. The chief exponent of those modes was the famous composer-poet Guillaume de Machaut, whose patrons were kings and princes. With what amounts to insolence Chaucer, in his early twenties and only just a king's esquire, wrote a poem in which, within a chime of echoes from a dozen or more other contemporary French poems, he redeployed large excerpts from poems by Machaut, undoubtedly known to his audience. And so that there should be no mistaking his intention, he opened his poem with a fifteen-line quotation from another poem in French, probably composed in England, by Jean Froissart the chronicler, who had been Queen Philippa's secretary from 1361 to 1366.

Englishmen before Chaucer had pillaged French verse for its content. None had set out as, from the openness of his quotations, Chaucer evidently did, to reproduce its effects of tone and sentiment in English, to rival it. For literary historians that intention marks a new stage in the development of English poetry, its opening made unmistakable by the completeness of Chaucer's success. His imitative, derivative poem is more densely textured than his French models, and therefore more interesting; it is more vital and therefore credible; and it is more musical—in short, better poetry. For Chaucer's audience, without our literary perspective, it will have seemed a calculated demonstration of the serviceability of the English language for the composition of fashionable poetry. This was something they might otherwise have questioned rather than taken for granted. Ten years later, that same John Gower was still writing long works in French and Latin.

The Book of the Duchess is overshadowed by Chaucer's later work, which seems more accessible and therefore more 'modern'. That response is not without significance; nevertheless, historically the *Duchess* is sensational—in 1368 there was nothing in England even remotely like it. Not that the country was an intellectual desert. As early as the twelfth century it had been the centre of a remarkable flowering of philosophical and literary culture, but in Latin. And from the later twelfth century on England had produced a considerable literature in Anglo-Norman, some so excellent that French literary historians claim it as part of their national heritage. Writings of distinction in English were produced in that period, but they are few, dispersed in time and various in nature and presumable intent. They clearly do not represent a literary tradition. Those which are cultivated and stylistically sophisticated probably record excursions into the vernacular by literati whose primary culture was Latin. Most pre-Chaucerian Middle English literature, apart from poems little known because of their difficult English that testify to an old but vital tradition of political and social satire, consists of relatively undistinguished reflexes of ecclesiastical Latin, or Anglo-Norman, or French models.

Some features of the strikingly novel excellence of the *Duchess* have to do with Chaucer's situation. For one thing, he was writing not as a professional entertainer of the minstrel class, a hack, but from within an audience whose ways and social idiom he knew, and about whose responses he could make assumptions valuable to him as a poet. For another, as a layman he had no preceptorial responsibility: he could address his audience naturally, not as from from pulpit or lectern, but as intellectual equals or superiors. Those circumstances ideally suited the accidents of his natural intelligence and his literary education at this point. The combination gives the *Duchess* a quality of urbanity, polish, which immediately distinguishes it from most previous Middle English poetry. The poem is polite literature as sophisticated as its French progenitors, not admonitory or rustic or provincial.

The narrator tells how, 'the other night', in a deep depression and unable to sleep—he has been hopelessly lovesick for eight years—he was reading Ovid's story of Ceyx and Alcyone. He describes their great love, how Ceyx was lost at sea, how Alcyone hearing no news of him became distraught, how Juno answering her prayer sent Morpheus the god of sleep with a vision of her husband's death, and how Alcyone died of grief. The narrator had not known of any god who could bestow sleep, but driven by his insomnia he made a vow of a gift to Morpheus and directly fell asleep over his book. He dreamed that he was in his own bed, wakened by glorious birdsong; then he heard the sounds of preparation for a stag-hunt; he was up and away after it in a moment. The chase faltered; there was a hound puppy that would not run, and it led him deep into a wood. There he came upon a young knight in black mourning. After civil exchanges the knight described how he loved a paragon of womanhood, telling of her peerless qualities, how at length she accepted his diffident proffer of love, how happy they were together, and how he lost her, by death. Now the huntsmen sounded the recall. The knight went home to a nearby castle; the dreamer awoke in the resolve to put his dream into the best verse he could contrive.

That bald account (the description of the lady and of the knight's courtship take up three-fifths of the text) cannot begin to suggest the radical novelty of the poem, its elegiac quality or, with respect to the poet's capabilities, how much it implied for Chaucer's career and the future of English literature.

First there is the extreme character of the innovation the poem constitutes as a reproduction in English of actual identifiable effects from known French poems. What lay behind Chaucer's decision to undertake this we can only speculate about. He may have been turned to English by a master at school. He may have initially written in English to please Queen Philippa who, as the daughter of the Count of Hainault, Holland and Zeeland, will not have had cause to love the French; or Blanche of Lancaster, who might have brought with her to court some of the Northern English hostility to French culture. Or he may have perceived that the French spoken in England, by now in effect a provincial dialect, was not a language to imitate Continental fashions in. Or he may, like Dante, have sensed and correctly valued the superior warmth and capacity to move of the language learned at the breast.

Then there was the finesse with which Chaucer exploited the huge range of emotional effects available in English from the dual ancestry of its vocabulary. It is a commonplace of language study to divide English vocabulary mainly into words of Saxon origin, relating to elemental but humble features of life, and those from Norman French and French, relating to warfare, professions, great affairs, elevated conceptions, high society. Chaucer's use of the language makes that distinction seem crude. He commanded not merely the archetypal resonances of the Saxon element, but also subtle differences of denotation and connotation in the imported words, those long naturalized or only recently imported, and those which a Londoner of his day might find it hard to classify with confidence as French or English. The innumerable fine differences of connotation in the composite vocabulary of Chaucer's English made it an exceptionally versatile poetic medium. Above all it was fresh, not ritually stylized as French had recently become through Machaut's eminence and the repetitive slightness of his poetic gift. The moment was right for someone of Chaucer's ability to develop the use of English while his own poetic insight grew with it. *The Book of the Duchess*, viewed in terms of previous Middle English verse, shows Chaucer well on the way.

Next there was the novelty of Chaucer playing the role of court poet, a performance that was part of his importation of the French mode. It was to please a succession of royal or princely patrons that Machaut, court poet *par excellence*, was composing his brilliant music and writing verse: this was his life. He was a professional entertainer, however distinguished as a composer, and his reward was a plurality of ecclesiastical sinecures. Similarly his contemporary the priest Froissart moved from court to court and wrote to please patrons. The main topic of these poets was love, and it was a required qualification for the court poet himself to be a lover. According to Machaut love poetry not written from actual experience was counterfeit. The English court had never had such a poet. And here now was a poem by that competent and promising young esquire, the one who had been in Navarre in '66 and had just come back from another mission abroad, in which the narrating voice, inevitably identified with him, described a hopeless lovesickness and referred to the unresponsive woman he loved as the only physician who could cure him, in a studied arrangement of unmistakable references to known French poems. Moreover the poem was 'about' real people. The dead lady's name, 'good, beautiful White', not one given to English women, suggested Blanche, and the 'long castle on a rich hill' to which the knight in black went home at the end of the dream confirmed the identification: Lancaster and Richmond were the titles of John of Gaunt. In the manner of court poetry the personages were idealized: the terms that described the lady's beauty came from at least twenty passages in four contemporary French poems; the knight was considerably younger than Gaunt; there was nothing about the daughter Gaunt fathered before he married Blanche, or the five children Blanche bore him before she died. Even the kind of love that consumed the young

27

knight was the elegant, ritualized sort the French poets wrote about; they called it *fine amour*, 'excellent love'. Gaunt's marriage to Blanche had in fact been arranged by his father to consolidate the kingship.

Chaucer's audience, Edward III's court, will not have failed to appreciate the novelty of the *Duchess* in all these particulars. But the poem is also significant in ways they cannot have foreseen.

Its peculiar genre, the dream-vision, was to shape Chaucer's poetic. Its distinctive features are simple. A speaker in the first person reports how, in spring and in a pleasant place, he fell asleep and dreamed, how in the dream he encountered a guide who led him to the main action of the dream, what this consisted of, then how some event within the dream awakened him, and how he resolved to put his remarkable experience into verse. French poets had, by Chaucer's time, developed that very elementary system of conventions into a serviceable poetic vehicle for topics ranging from erotic or frivolous to moral and spiritual. Two of the developments are relevant here.

The first was their use of it for allegorical, that is, more than literal meaning. This was encouraged by Old Testament accounts of dream divinations, by a treatise on dreams embodied in a post-classical commentary by Macrobius on Book VI of Cicero's *Republic*, known as *Somnium Scipionis*, 'Scipio's Vision', and by the natural interest in dreams as a form of experience. By Chaucer's time one of the expectations set up by the dream-vision genre was of some deeper meaning than the literal. Poems in the genre challenged interpretation. It was for Chaucer's audience to perceive analogies between the situation of Ceyx and Alcyone and that of 'good, beautiful White' and her knight, then between those two and Blanche and Gaunt. The poem invited consideration of what the three pairs of lovers, two described and one suggested, had in common and how they differed. From the dream-vision Chaucer learned to claim the co-operation of his audience, and he did this with increasing importunity for the rest of his poetic career, developing literary situations of progressively greater challenge from which, at least ostensibly, he, the poet, withdrew further and further.

The second development had to do with the identity of the narrator of the dream. Because of his claim to have experienced the dream, this was a personal, intimate genre. The narrator was in the poem, always as observer, generally more actively. His narrating voice, meanwhile, seemed to be the poet's voice, and at the end he might claim authorship. If he had a name it was the poet's; in some dream-visions he had historically verifiable attributes of the poet. But because the dream reported was fiction, the dreamer as observer, reporter and participant was also a fiction, created by the historical poet. There may have been an implication of identity between narrator and poet, but the content of the poem cautioned against this: thus the poet further engaged interest. Chaucer sensed the possibilities of this situation at the outset. The dreamer of the *Duchess* is obtuse in not at once perceiving the reason for the knight's grief, responds clownishly to classical legend, has not heard of the gods of the pantheon. He is one of the puppets manipulated by the poet, who wrote all the parts. In that character he is a device enabling Chaucer to accommodate the discrepancies between his public images as a serious and competent royal servant and as a writer committed to the postures and attitudes of the court poet. He is the progenitor of the first-person narrators in Chaucer's subsequent works who will be main agents of meaning because the audience cannot trust their judgement and must therefore exercise its own.

Chaucer never again wrote seriously as a court poet. But the experience played a part in forming both his own conception of himself as a poet, and his attitude to his audience. He had by 1370 correctly assessed his own capabilities and discovered where he stood with associates and superiors; and he sensed his power as a poet. So he had two worlds, one that of great affairs in which his place, though not contemptible, was circumscribed, the other of the mind, his own to the limit of his talent. For discrete reasons he was committed to both, and they were incompatible; indeed the discrepancy between them would grow with his learning and poetic skills. He would turn it to account by distorting it, in various representations of 'himself the poet', the speaker of his poems, as the dedicated poet of lovers denied success in love, as devoid of sensibility, as imperceptive, lacking in judgement. His audience, knowing him, would soon perceive that this was more than coterie humour, and would identify what they knew as the posture of the *fol sage*, the 'wise fool' or ironist.

That audience, drawn from the king's court, great households like Gaunt's, and London, was highly various, stratified both socially and culturally. It comprised aristocrats of cultivation in increasing numbers, knights of the royal household, some themselves minor poets, royal servants like Chaucer, lawyers, divines, merchants. All would have some degree of literary cultivation in Latin and French, and were probably acquainted with English popular verse. Their literary sophistication would grow with Chaucer's developing command of his art.

The Book of the Duchess was Chaucer's last considerable imitation of French court poetry. He undoubtedly
sensed that he had surpassed his models, but insight into
their shallowness and lack of implication will have
made that seem a limited achievement. His next long
poem shows him with a larger objective, suggested by
new models he found in Italian poetry.

Nevertheless he continued in debt to France. He used
the socially elegant tones of Machaut and Froissart
where appropriate in the dramatic narratives to the
composition of which he principally devoted himself in
his mature years. A part of his cultural education was to
translate the *Roman de la Rose*, a long thirteenth-
century French poem by two successive authors a
generation apart, begun as an elegantly witty erotic
allegory, and completed as an extended commentary on
humbug and pretence, but with a paradoxical foundation
of satirical idealism. He drew upon this all his days. He
made frequent and extensive use of French vernacular
scholarship, especially translations of Latin and even
Italian texts, and French commentaries on Ovid. He
evidently admired and occasionally reproduced in English
the astringent social criticism of Eustace Deschamps, who
for his part identified the philosophical strain in Chaucer's
writings, and paid Chaucer the ultimate compliment
possible at that time from a French poet to an English
one, of addressing him in an effusively laudatory poem.
French culture of the great period from 1150 to 1300,
though it never produced a major poet, can claim
Chaucer as one of its signal achievements.

Paris was the intellectual centre of Europe when
Dante was writing, and its culture was scholastic and
Latin. By 1370 the centre had shifted to Northern Italy.
Here its most distinguished expression was in the

vernacular. The base of this new culture was still Latin, but its design was different: it was no loger primarily theological, but humanistic. The learning underlying the Latin writings of Petrarch and Boccaccio was that of classical antiquity, to which those men saw themselves as successors.

We do not know when it was that Chaucer, by learning Italian, won access to the poetry of these men and their master Dante. Languages came easily to the highly developed memories of those times, and London afforded ready opportunity. It was a main trading-port for Italian shipping. There were Italians high in the king's service: even the royal moneyer, a successor of Chaucer's maternal great-uncle, was Italian, a Bardi of the Florentine banking family associated with the crown since the time of Edward I. Indeed the first husband of Dante's Beatrice Portinari had been a Bardi. These were northerners from Dante country: it is barely conceivable that Chaucer failed to hear about him from such people. It may have been their accounts of the already famous *Commedia* that set him to learning the language, if perceiving its advantages in the service was not induce-ment enough. He was certainly fluent in Italian by 1372 when he was sent to Genoa as the one Englishman on a mission with two native Italians. Of course they knew English, but to be of any use for surveillance and report Chaucer had to be able to understand them speaking quickly to each other in dialect. When that mission was completed he went on without them to Florence.

That journey was above all an opportunity to acquire Italian books. The importance of what Chaucer found in these can hardly be exaggerated. His first experience of Italian poetry seems to have been the *Divine Comedy*. That will have brought home to him the limitations of the fourteenth-century French court poetry he had mastered, its narrow intellectual dimensions, diffuseness and attenuated emotion. The career of Dante, who was being talked and written about in terms previously reserved for the giants of antiquity, showed him what stature a vernacular poet could attain, suggesting new scope for his own achievement. And Dante had written, not, like Machaut and Froissart, as a truant priest about frivolities, but as a layman with hard experience of the world, of matters deeply devout. Reading the *Divine Comedy* enlarged Chaucer's conception of poetry and the poet. To this the work and careers of Petrarch and Boccacio further contributed both a kind of self-conscious glamour and a greatly extended historical perspective.

The first effect of that experience shows in *The House of Fame*, an unfinished poem that resists critical interpretation, but, by the intense intellectual and creative excitement it registers, is an unmistakable landmark in his career.

A man dreams that he is in a temple of glass dedicated to Venus, full of antique pictures and statuary. On one wall there is a tablet of brass on which is engraved the story of Dido and Aeneas, set in an account of his career of destiny. Coming out of the temple the dreamer finds himself in a vast desert. At once a huge eagle, bright gold like a second sun, seizes and bears him up into the sky. This is a messenger of Jove, directed, he tells the dreamer, whom he calls Geffrey, to take him to a palace, the house of Fame. That is Jove's recompense to him for long and arduous but hitherto unrewarded literary services to the God of Love and his mother. He will now see incredibly many and various marvels and 'tidynges' (happenings) to do with lovers and love. How did these all come to the house of Fame? The eagle explains in a lecture on the physics of sound. As they soar he offers another on astronomy, but the dreamer declines it, and they arrive. The house of Fame is a splendid castle intricately built of seamless beryl. All around outside are entertainers of every sort, minstrels, story-tellers, magicians and conjurers. Inside is the goddess Fame: in Middle English the word signifies good *or* bad repute. She has innumerable eyes and ears and tongues; her stature varies hugely. Alexander and Hercules sit on her shoulders; the nine Muses, singing, surround her throne. From that throne to the broad doors stretch two rows of pillars on which stand historians and poets notable for having caused notable men and events to be remembered. To the goddess comes group after group of suppliants; to each without regard to what they ask, or to desert, capriciously she awards good fame or bad or oblivion. This is not what the dreamer came to see, not 'tidynges' of love. An affable man in the temple who addresses him, 'Are you one of the petitioners?', puts him right. Hard by at the foot of the castle hill is a structure shaped like a cage, sixty miles in diameter, built of wickerwork, revolving with the speed of thought. Luckily the eagle happens to be handy, to help the dreamer in. And there he finds an uncountable crowd, each person whispering in another's ear. Rumour is magnified, true and false are inextricably linked. In a corner there is a dense, noisy, jostling press of people, where 'love-tidynges' are being told. The dreamer catches sight of a man he cannot name, who seems to be highly reliable. The poem breaks off.

That abstract suggests its imaginative scale. We cannot know how, had Chaucer finished the poem, he would have brought together, into a single meaningful structure, its three disparate and disproportionate books.

But the poem unmistakably communicates exuberant energy. Chaucer's imagination, fired by the *Divine Comedy*, had broken out of the French confines. Dante showed him cosmic dimensions and an eagle as a means of travelling in them. Ovid's *Metamorphoses* provided the house of rumour, his *Heroides* the pathetic Dido. Dante's range of reference excited Chaucer: his emulation of it shows how much he had read since 1369. There are slips: apparently he did not know that Chiron was a centaur; misled by an Italian spelling, he took the satyr Marsyas for a woman; a scribal error in a manuscript quotation from Horace by John of Salisbury led him to think that there was a Latin historian of the Trojan war called Lollius. But what mattered was his excitement with learning, with the association with antiquity and the enterprise it engendered. As if defiantly, he translates the opening of the *Aeneid*,

> I wol now singen, yif I kan,
> The armes, and also the man
> That first cam, thurgh his destinee,
> Fugityf of Troy contree,
> In Itayle, with ful moche pyne
> Unto the strondes of Lavyne. (283)

> Now, if I can, I mean to sing of deeds of arms and the man, a fugitive from the Trojan land, whose destiny brought him after much hardship, as a leader, to Italy and the shores of Lavinium.

And then he rejects Virgil's version of the Dido story for Ovid's, which he tells with a pointed elegance new in English poetry.

The *Commedia* showed Chaucer the high seriousness of poetry and the intensity of the poet's engagement. The *Commedia* was about ultimate issues, its style constantly vibrant with intellectual energy registered in linguistic tension. It was not seldom 'sublime'; Chaucer did not have that conveniently vague term to describe poetic experience so moving as to transport the reader, but he identified and could imitate the Dantean high style. By contrast the substance of Machaut's poetry was social triviality, and the manner undistinguished.

Dante's conception of himself as poet was a revelation. Both Dante and Machaut had egos that still dominate their works: that is the extent of the resemblance. The difference in the expression of those egos is absolute. It lies in the circumstance that Machaut, as court poet, had by his own prescription to be Machaut the lover. He plays that part at length in one work which he names *Le Voir Dit*, 'The Poem with a True Story', where he figures as a protagonist. This is presented as an open diary of a love affair between the poet, in his fifties, and a young gentlewoman of eighteen who writes verses. Its kind of seriousness can be gauged from the elderly lover complaining that the warfare and freebooting which were turning his country into a desert made travelling to visit one's mistress difficult. Dante had another view of the poet's, in effect his own, standing. This he recorded in the fourth book of the *Inferno* where the great ancients, Homer, Horace, Ovid and Lucan, after conferring with Virgil, conclude to make him the sixth in their company. And they all walk together for a time, speaking of arcane matters.

Such absolute difference would make Chaucer consider his own situation. The country was full of those love-songs of his youth; now he was drawn to the Dantean mode. If he attempted to reproduce it he would be seen to take himself seriously as a poet. Meanwhile everyone in the small world of court and London officialdom had known him since he was a boy. If, as all indications suggest, he was a deeply serious person with a sense of the ridiculous so acute that he found it hard to strike solemn postures, let alone maintain them, this was a situation calculated to make him highly self-conscious. He must conceal the depth of his engagement to poetry, his sense of his own capability.

The House of Fame registers Chaucer's problem of his identity as a poet. One signal is inconsistencies of tone and practice. The poem opens with a succession of discords. The dreamer asserts that his was the most marvellous dream ever experienced, by way of a belittling glance at the meanings of six different terms for dream and a dismissive list of fifteen physical or psychological reasons why people dream. He solemnly invokes the God of Sleep whom Chaucer had with pointed self-consciousness introduced into *The Book of the Duchess*, the first poem in English with Olympian deities as personages. Then in the next breath, echoing the last line of Dante's *Paradiso*, the dreamer prays to 'Him that movere ys of al' (God in whom all things originate). But the prayer is not for his soul: he asks God to further the love-suits or other pursuits of those who hear his poem. Then, admitting a failure of charity, he invokes misfortune on anyone who misinterprets it. The reason for his flight with the eagle is ludicrous, his invocation to Apollo, 'god of science and of light' (of learning and enlightenment), deadly serious. Such fluctuations reflect Chaucer's state of mind, experimental, still lacking full critical self-assurance and a sense of direction. Nevertheless some features of his poetic identity are already fully formed: it is taking shape. In representing the dreamer as an inept lover Chaucer pointedly distanced himself from Machaut's 'Qui de sentement ne

fait Son dit et son chant contrefait' (the poet who writes
of love without direct experience composes false verse
and false music). And the invocations are studied echoes
of those in the *Commedia* at the beginning of the
descent into Hell and the ascent into Paradise. The trend
of development is clear enough.

The immediate product of the self-mockery generated
in this situation was comedy, realized in the condescen-
sion of the eagle to Geffrey—'You have done your best
with such intelligence as you have'—and his reasons for
sympathizing with him:

> 'when thy labour doon al ys,
> And hast mad alle thy rekenynges,
> In stede of reste and newe thynges,
> Thou goost hom to thy hous anoon;
> And also domb as any stoon,
> Thou sittest at another book
> Tyl fully daswed ys thy look.' (288)

'When your work is all done and you have completed
your accounting, instead of rest and a change you go
straight home and sit over another book as dumb as a
stone, until you have quite blinded yourself.'

The second product is the establishment of an ironic
relation between poet and audience. Those who knew
only the French court poetry which Chaucer replicated
in the *Duchess* might see him in the Geffrey to whom
the eagle condescended. The perceptive correctly ap-
preciated the circumstance that it was the Chaucer
known to them who had arranged the language by which
this imaginary situation existed. Possibly none understood the additional significance: that this was an act of
self-assurance in which the poet dramatized his sense of

his own distinctiveness. For the literary finesse with which the actual Chaucer made comic capital of the anomaly of his situation, turned it to advantage, abolished the anomaly for himself. In his mind the outlines of the different Chaucers, king's esquire and responsible official, secret scholar ambitious to attain the standing of Dante, and aspiring poet, grew faint; they merged in the privacy of his unsharable thoughts, into a complex, secret personality.

This is the beginning of a development which shaped Chaucer's theory and practice of poetry. In *The House of Fame* the self-mockery began as a protective screen, to hide the excitement of the poet about a new kind of poetry, and himself as a new kind of person, which he feared might not be understood. In the immediate context of the eagle's ponderous mockery and the search for love-tidings it can be read as part of the ineffectuality of the dreamer. But the poem has one passage which, just conceivably without Chaucer realizing, is a formula for the irony to come. Geffrey is turning away disappointed from the house of Fame, and just by him there is the friendly stranger who asks him civilly whether he is there as a petitioner for fame. 'Indeed, no,' Geffrey answers,

> 'I cam noght hyder, graunt mercy,
> For no such cause, by my hed!
> Sufficeth me, as I were ded,
> That no wight have my name in honde.
> I wot myself best how y stonde;
> For what I drye, or what I thynke,
> I wil myselven al hyt drynke,
> Certeyn, for the more part,
> As fer forth as I kan myn art.' (299–300)

39

'You are most kind to ask, but I swear I came here for no such reason. It is enough for me—supposing I were dead—that no one should bandy my name about. I am the one who knows best how I am placed. Whatever I may feel deeply, or may think, I am resolved to keep it all—most of it, be sure of that, to myself, to the extent that I know how to exercise my particular gifts and education.'

One unmistakable subject of Chaucer's *House of Fame* is himself as poet. The work communicates his preoccupation with the discovery of what he could achieve, and his aspirations. From the subconscious stored by those long nights of solitary reading comes the insight, that which was 'ymarked' (imprinted) in his head, what he needed Apollo's divine power to help him realize. Words flowed from his pen, creating a radically new effect, a remarkably visual, surrealistic represent-ation of what never was and was never seen. He caught the tones of the human voice; without English models he hit upon comedy, and the exquisite pleasure of playing a comic role in his own work. But he was uneasy about being misread, about his 'lyght and lewed' (slight and vulgar) metre (292). And his control of form was insecure. The essentially shapeless dream-vision genre had not trained him to match or even approach the fearful symmetry of the *Commedia*; the last of his three books is nearly as long as the first two together, and this made him uncomfortable. He was very self-conscious about the whole business. We shall never see Chaucer reveal himself like this again.

His other subject was truth, of both report and poetry. This the third book openly addresses, but it is implicit in the story of Dido engraved on the brass tablets in the temple of Book I. Chaucer knew two versions of her story, Virgil's in the *Aeneid*, where Aeneas is driven to leave her by the gods and his destiny as the founder of Rome, the other Ovid's in the *Heroides*, where Aeneas is a dastardly philanderer who takes advantage of and heartlessly deserts her. The text on the wall tells the story of Ovid's pathetic Dido as if Chaucer had made an empirical choice between likelihoods. Worse still, two scholars, an Englishman in the 1320s and Petrarch about a decade later, had shown the historical impossibility of Dido and Aeneas ever meeting: her name was even used to denote a story of no credence, a minstrel's tale. Here then were three truths: that of political support in Virgil's version, the English equivalent being the twelfth-century fabrication that the Trojans had founded Britain; that of observed experience—men do behave badly to women, do make them wretched; and the actuality of history. In the spinning wickerwork house Geffrey sees a lie and a solid truth arrive together at a window, both wanting out. Neither will give way: they shove and shout. The upshot is that they become inseparable. Nobody shall have one without the other, true and false will be compounded in a single report. Concern about truth, and its expression in human conduct as integrity, would become a main element in Chaucer's later poetry. That concern was refined during the obsessive reading Chaucer lets us glimpse in the unique intimacy of this one poem about himself.

3 New horizons

How avidly Chaucer read shows from the increasing
depth and range of literary reference, open or unacknow-
ledged, in his successive works. He can be seen emerging
into a world of perspectives reaching to the learning and
poetry of antiquity. Some of its magnitude he must have
glimpsed as a schoolboy, since at that time even a junior
London school, like the St Paul's Almonry School,
would have works by half a dozen major Latin poets.
They were also extensively quoted in both the Latin
grammars from which boys were taught. Books that will
have increased his sense of the extent of ancient
literature were Richard of Bury's *Philobiblon*, 'The
Booklover', and Walter Burley's *Lives and Customs of
the Philosophers.*

But nothing in Chaucer's experience can have affected
his relation to the classical past more than Dante's
account of those five great poets of antiquity taking him
unto themselves. And at some time after writing *The
House of Fame*, that is after 1374, possibly not until his
second Italian journey in 1378, he came upon works by
Petrarch and Boccaccio, and, in them, the first expressions of humanism. Unlike Dante, whose intellectual
affinities were with a scholastic philosophy already
moribund when he glorified it in the *Divine Comedy*,
these two personified the beginnings of an erudite
culture which turned for guidance and models back to
the actual texts of classical antiquity, but in full
confidence of the status of its own vernacular poetry.
Dante had shown Chaucer (and them) what heights such

poetry could reach. Petrarch and Boccaccio in turn showed Chaucer, as had the French poets, how he could learn from men of lesser talent and superior cultivation. Above all they taught him a new idea of a poet.

Chaucer's respect for Dante can be gauged from the closeness of some half-dozen large, studied imitations of his exalted or solemn style, not to mention a great many smaller echoes or quotations. But their mentalities and situations differed extremely. One reason was the difference of their worlds. The cluster of urban oligarchies in which Dante played for power was calculated to embitter its failures by the intimacy of the rivalry. In Chaucer's world the rules of the game were different. He belonged to a nation that had just attained self-respect, not to a city that had rejected him. Politics from the financial to the dynastic seethed around him, but they were still shaped in a feudal ethic that only extreme radicals like the peasant leaders of 1381 or Wyclif disputed. Chaucer's disappointment was not, like Dante's, with a small community that had turned on him, but with the personality of a king. And in his world factions were not hard but fluctuating; realignment was frequent according to notions of the good government of the realm.

Another difference is chronological. Dante, writing in the last days of scholastic Aristotelianism, the attempt to put Aristotle's physics and metaphysics to the service of Christian doctrine, could still propose in the *Convivio* (1304–8) that man's intelligence was capable of access to the spiritual world, and that he could gain by speculative philosophy significant understanding of supernatural truths. That proposition enabled him to avoid the eschatological predicament of medieval Christianity by rationalizing it in ways that might seem unacceptable to a cold logical eye. By Chaucer's time the repeated prohibitions of speculative philosophy issued by the ecclesiastical hierarchy of Paris, notably the comprehensive ones of 1270 and 1277, 'Let not Aristotle's books of metaphysics and natural philosophy be read' because 'the spirit of Christ does not reign where Aristotelian enquiry prevails', had exercised their full, stultifying effect. Chaucer's philosophical excursions were to be in the two areas left by the prohibitions, namely epistemology, the redefinition of terms designed to reduce the appearance of irrationality of received dogma, and moral philosophy, which, because dogmatic answers existed to moral questions, had been of lesser interest to the school philosophers in the universities. The translation of Boethius's *Consolation of Philosophy*, which Chaucer undertook in the 1380s, constituted a strenuous exercise in epistemology, and there is no sign that Chaucer found this in itself rewarding. He did respond to the Neoplatonism in the *Consolation*, which was in a sense already known to him through its Christian form as the concept of divine love. Chaucer's mind was drier than Dante's, and he had a superior mathematical aptitude, which he presently developed to the point of becoming a practical astronomer.

They also differed radically in their early experience of poetry. This was in both cases love poetry, that is, poetry addressed to a woman in attitudes conventionally prescribed. But the forms of prescription were not identical and the quality differed. Love poetry came to Dante from Provence, both directly (the Italians were great collectors of Provençal lyrics) and as it had been Italianized in Sicily by learned amateurs. The Italian form was refined in the generation before Dante, enriched with scientific and metaphysical correlatives. And the Italians who carried out this process wrote not for patrons but for each other as equal and competing members of a group. It came to Chaucer mainly from the *Roman de la Rose*, either directly or in the writings of French court poets who were also clerics, thus at the outset to some degree compromised, and always posturing. Dante's luck was to be able to spiritualize, Platonize the original Provençal attitudes. By contrast Chaucer's poetry exhibits a progressively stronger revulsion from idealization of the sex relationship, a sense of the bankruptcy of a poetic mode at best declined into frivolity, at worst spurious, and it suggests a contempt for Machaut.

One further difference was in their experiences of the physical world, which were of kinds to leave the dogmatic assurance of the one untroubled and to encourage the other in open pragmatism. It is very doubtful whether Dante ever left Italy or travelled farther south than Rome; Chaucer first crossed the Channel at fourteen. He learned about distance on the Bay of Biscay, the mountain tracks of Navarre, the long route to Italy by way of the Low Countries and Germany. Both heard the talk of the Genoese navigators, but Chaucer knew the force of Atlantic gales. Dante's geography, erudite enough, was bookish and theoretical. Chaucer's had been physically experienced as seasickness, saddle-stiffness, surly natives, fleas in bad inns. 'Of course we must believe what we read in books,' he wrote in the late 1380s (in the *Prologue* to *The Legend of Good Women*). Not everything can be tested, and where would we be without what books tell us about the past? Nevertheless

> ther nis noon dwellyng in this contree,
> That eyther hath in hevene or helle ybe, (482)

There is no one living in this country who has been in either heaven or hell.

With Petrarch Chaucer's relation as a poet was simpler and more direct. They could have met in early 1373, but we have no evidence that they did. The Clerk on the Canterbury pilgrimage tells a story that very closely reproduces a Latin prose narrative of Petrarch's, which he called 'Concerning Fabulous Wifely Obedience and Constancy', the folk-tale of Patient Grizzle. And Troilus, early in the course of his destructive passion for Criseyde, is made to compose a 'song' of three seven-line stanzas which closely translate a Petrarcan sonnet. Such deft application implies that Chaucer knew enough of Petrarch's work to have a choice. But his use is not straightforward, and has a critical element. Chaucer's Clerk tells how he learned his story in Padua from the laureate Petrarch, 'whose sweet rhetoric filled all Italy with the light of poetry'. But he dims the glory of that praise by adding a matching eulogy of a professor of canon law. And the Clerk is critical of the opening section of Petrarch's story, although it is actually an elaborate rhetorical figure called *topographia* (the introduction of geographical description in narrative); it seems an irrelevancy to him. As for the sonnet assigned to Troilus, it is one of many spoken as by Petrarch in his own person; to judge by Chaucer's use of it he thought it more appropriately expressive of emotionally disturbed adolescence than the state of mind of a middle-aged cleric. Petrarch told his Griselda story as an exemplum of submission to God's will; Chaucer exploited its outrageous quality in a dramatic conflict between feminist and antifeminist points of view. The sense of these adaptations is that Chaucer saw in Petrarch an artist well within his own range, to be emulated and outdone.

With Boccaccio Chaucer's literary relation was extensive, close, and altogether enigmatic. He took or used more from Boccaccio than from either of the other Italians. He knew Boccaccio's *Filostrato, Filocolo* and *Teseida,* and his three encylopaedic Latin works, *The Disastrous Careers of Famous Men, Illustrious Women* and *The Genealogy of the Pagan Gods.* He based the central element of his first venture into moral philosophy, *The Parlement of Foules,* on a Boccaccian passage and its author's commentary. And the plots of his *Knight's Tale* and *Troilus and Criseyde* are Boccaccian. He echoed, in effect quoted, Boccaccio without acknowledgement, countless times. He mastered and very skilfully naturalized in English the distinguished grace and elegance of Boccaccio's youthful style, and plundered the erudition of his later years. For Chaucer Boccaccio's works were a repository of motifs, models of rich and elaborate systems of rhetoric and style, a port of entry into the antique world, a liberal education.

But Chaucer never made any acknowledgement, never so much as named Boccaccio. Indeed he invented a fiction that the source of his *Troilus and Criseyde,* for which Boccaccio's *Filostrato* had provided the story, was that non-existent Latin historian of Troy, Lollius; and once, in *The Monk's Tale,* where Chaucer drew on Boccaccio he implied that his source was Petrarch. Even when Chaucer first went to Italy Boccaccio was a prominent literary figure. Within a few months of Chaucer's departure he was asked to inaugurate a foundation of Dante lectures. It is virtually impossible that Chaucer did not know who wrote the works he plundered. So the notion of something behind Chaucer's suppression of Boccaccio's name is hard to dismiss and the temptation to speculate is powerful. What comes immediately to mind is that they met and Boccaccio behaved condescendingly, possibly corrected Chaucer's mistaken notion about Lollius. Or the explanation may simply be the notorious 'rigoglio dei Fiorentini', Florentine brashness. Chaucer may even have been angered by Boccaccio's description of the English in his *Disastrous Careers* as 'most sluggish and timorous and worthless people'.

With Chaucer's discovery of the rank of his talent there went the acquisition of a new idea of a poet. To this he was highly receptive simply from the self-consciousness implicit in his situation as a writer in the vernacular. It was in Italy, partly from Dante's example and partly through the erudite enthusiasm of the Boccaccio whom Chaucer consumed, that a radically new standing for vernacular poets was asserted. Boccaccio formulated it, defending poetry against moralistic attacks, in a controversial chapter of *The Genealogy of the Pagan Gods*. The formulation is put together with a fine philosophical instinct from asides and single statements in the available works of Cicero and Horace, as well as of transmitters like Macrobius, Augustine and the encyclopaedist Isidore of Seville.

A poet was the rarest of beings. What drove him to composition was a frenzy, in Boccaccio's Latin, *fervor*; here is the concept 'inspiration'. A vernacular poet could immortalize himself just as the ancients had done; he belonged to a tradition that stemmed from them. This was heady stuff, but it was soberly backed up. Merely the impulse does not make a commendable poet. He must have an abundant vocabulary, be a master of grammar and rhetoric, be conversant with both moral and natural philosophy (that is, natural science), be knowledgeable about history and geography, and be aware of the 'monuments and relics' of antiquity.

One of the novelties of this idea of a poet was its secular character. Boccaccio saw the moral function of poetry not from the commonplace viewpoint of medieval criticism as a religious responsibility, but in a perspective that reached to the classical past as a responsibility to its own essential nature as a repository of truth. The erudition Boccaccio prescribed amounted to the difference between 'wanting to write' and 'having something to say'. It would particularize the *fervor*, confer shape and substance and more general implication on the writer's response to observed experience. In terms of literary history Boccaccio was proclaiming the poet to be not an entertainer but a man of letters, a philosopher.

There is no way of proving that Chaucer actually saw the chapter in Boccaccio's *Genealogy* where the idea of a poet is shaped, but his career after *The House of Fame* can be read as a systematic realization of it, as if, in the words of Petrarch when he received the laurel crown in 1341, he would not wish to seem a poet and nothing more. Chaucer became, in his middle years, immensely learned, so much so that hunting down his allusions has occupied three generations of academics, and it may yet be more. The obsessive reading he seems to attribute to himself, as if in self-mockery, in the *House of Fame*, to judge by the depth and breadth of reference in his subsequent works, became a way of life.

He undoubtedly collected books. One of his self-projections, in the 1394 *Prologue* to *The Legend of Good Women*, is said to own 'sixty bokes olde and newe' (490). The figure is unlikely to be exact, but it undoubtedly signifies 'very many'; to go by the numbers of books mentioned in the wills of contemporary and later people of great wealth and substance, it amounts to a considerable collection, bespeaking exceptional interest, exertion and expenditure on the part of its owner. Chaucer also had access to great libraries. In London alone there were the ancient collections of the cathedral library of St Paul's, of the Abbey of St Peter at Westminster, of the Charterhouse, and of the Austin Priory of St Bartholomew's Smithfield, repositories of the erudition of twelfth- and thirteenth-century monasticism; and the more modern libraries of the five orders of friars, notably that of the Dominicans, reflecting the intellectually advanced, sometimes radical, thinking of the fraternal orders at their best.

Chaucer was not a professional Latinist. The texts of classical writings available in his time had no apparatus of notes and glossary such as we rely on nowadays, and there was no systematic Latin dictionary. A work was likely to be encrusted with commentary, more often allegorizing, devoted to adapting its paganism to a Christian meaning, rather than elucidatory. Like any sensible man Chaucer used translations of the classical texts. The great recovery of the literature of antiquity was only just beginning, and his works mention writers who were not yet available in the England of his time. But there were excellent books of selections, scholarly compilations of the late thirteenth and early fourteenth centuries, that increased the accessibility of ancient literature.

As for philosophy, there existed a number of very substantial commonplace books and epitomes of classical thought. Most were anonymous, but the names of two notable compilers are known: one the Walter Burley earlier mentioned, who died in 1345, having been student of Duns Scotus, commentator on Aristotle, almoner to Edward's Queen Philippa, and tutor to the Black Prince; the other John of Wales (the better scholar), who had been regent master, that is, in charge of certain kinds of teaching, at Oxford about 1360. Wales's compilation, representing the best learning of his time, is fundamentally eclectic and syncretic, set down without evident Christian dogmatic bias.

Some of the cosmology of Plato's *Timaeus* came to Chaucer in two long Latin poems by Alain de Lille, a twelfth-century monk of Chartres. He was immersed in Platonic thought while translating Boethius's *Consolation of Philosophy*. Speculative Aristotelian metaphysics were denied to his time by the edicts of the Parisian hierarchy a century earlier, but he found a courageous recommendation of the hypothesis as an instrument of thought in John of Salisbury's *Metalogicon*. Among moral philosophers Seneca had a special position in the Middle Ages. In sub-theology he had the standing of a Christian saint, many of his teachings having been assimilated into early Christianity. Chaucer need not have seen a manuscript of Seneca's writings: all the Stoicism he shows knowledge of, exclusively ethical and mainly concerned with self-regulation and excessive attachment to worldly concerns, could have come from John of Wales's compilations. The philosophy most congenial to Chaucer seems to have been the ethically biased eclecticism instanced by Cicero in his *De Officiis* and the last book of the *Republic*, known in Chaucer's time as the text for Macrobius's treatise on dreams. Chaucer's access to the ancient philosophers by way of compendia and epitomes was not altogether disadvantageous. He was spared the frustration of using unedited, corrupt texts of their works, without scholarly apparatus.

And as an amateur he benefited from the compilers'
synopses and eclecticism: the best of them had a very
highly developed sense of salience, and this may even
have enhanced the reductive power of Chaucer's own
intelligence, which can be seen in critical action when
he represents extreme philosophical positions.

In the spirit of Boccaccio's poet as natural philosopher,
Chaucer turned mainly to two encyclopaedic works
compiled in the mid-thirteenth century, miscellanies of
almost all the scientific, quasi-scientific and pseudo-
scientific knowledge available in Europe at that time:
the *Speculum Maius* or 'Greater Mirror' of Vincent of
Beauvais, and Bartholomew the Englishman's *De Pro-
prietatibus Rerum*, 'The Properties of Entities and
Substances'. In one field of science, mathematics, his
knowledge was more than just derivative. His skill at
computation is implied by his work both as Controller
and as Clerk of the Works; he developed this by the
application of mathematics to observational astronomy,
which he expressed in his *Treatise on the Astrolabe*,
written in 1391 for his ten-year-old son Lewis. This is an
efficient manual, not an original scientific study, which
draws on two Latin technical works. But he could not
have understood them or written it without a solid
background in mathematics. The easy style of his prose
shows him to have been quite comfortable in the
undertaking.

Already by 1380 when Chaucer was nearing or had
reached his middle thirties his peculiar combination of
experience and abilities, what he called, in the *Introduction* to *The Pardoner's Tale*, the 'gifts of Fortune and
of Nature' (148), had made him a very complex personality. He had two public images, of the royal servant of
proven efficiency and discretion, and of the original and

gifted poet who had shown that English was a serviceable language for the art. The situation contained an implication of dual identity. In the public eye the poetry must necessarily have appeared his secondary concern, an eccentric if clever avocation. But from the expense of energy implied in his works it is clear that in Chaucer's private conception of himself the relation of the two roles, the two classes of activity, was inverse, although he carefully masked the situation. The identity projected by the speaking voice in his poetry and the one we must infer from the historical records of his career differ absolutely, in both their natures and their modes of existence. One is a contrivance brought into being by calculated arrangements of language, the other exists by virtue of a succession of historical events. They are so diverse that we would never come anywhere near to guessing the historical Chaucer from the voice that speaks in his poetry.

The situation was further complicated by the circumstance that the image of the young man with a talent for poetry concealed Chaucer's development into a man of letters, a scholar-poet. In a sense he was leading two lives, one as an energetically appetitive intellect fulfilling itself by addictive reading and compulsive writing, the other occupied with tactical understanding of his associates, what amounted to a pragmatic study of human behaviour.

But whatever the danger here of dichotomy, of the intellectual withdrawal into a literary world, this did not materialize. It is clear from the developed insight into men's motives and values evinced in his mature work that Chaucer did not separate the two classes of experience. Indeed several forces joined to complete his understanding of the essential nature of poetry by showing him human behaviour as its primary subject.

There was, first, his own early education in canonical morality, evidently rigorous and extensive. Second, there was the currency of a body of literature, in both Latin and the vernaculars, which formulated that morality into systematic criticisms of the conduct of members of almost all occupations or classes of society. That literature, nowadays called 'estates satire', simply by existing as a scheme of concepts for organizing observation of individual behaviour, prompted attention to this: people were sensitized to the morality of others. Third, all medieval poetic theory asserted the concern of the art with morality: poetry was actually classified as a branch of moral philosophy, its subject 'the behaviour of men'. Above all, Chaucer's living and working in a stratum of society where the two drives, for money as a symbol of security or power, and for physical gratification, were least subject to external checks, afforded exceptional opportunity for observing the starkness of the opposition between those elemental instincts and the canonical moral imperatives.

Occasionally Chaucer's earlier works suggest the poet in search of a subject. His life and times duly provided this. What came, from his observed experience, to obsess him, was the human condition seen in terms of necessary choice between apparently conflicting values, the relation of individual personality to the choice made, and the effect of choice upon personality: why people behave as they do and how they come to be as they are. Because of its immense spiritual implications that subject was absolutely serious: that justified Chaucer's gratification of his other obsession, writing, the arrangement of language into satisfying forms, that is, poetry. His insight deepened and his command of his art grew in combination, and there developed out of them a poetry of the highest order that can truly be said to belong to moral philosophy.

The seriousness of Chaucer's concern with behaviour would be confirmed by the time and energy he devoted to translating texts on moral subjects. An early translation, now lost, was of a treatise on Mary Magdalene attributed to the third-century Greek Church Father Origen. Another probably early one was of the *Roman de la Rose*, a huge poem that conceals immensely learned philosophical concern under a surface of cynically anticlerical and anticanonical eroticism. Some of this translation has survived, as has Chaucer's entire translation of Boethius's *Consolation of Philosophy*, probably made between 1386 and 1389, the first into English after King Alfred's. He also, late in his career, translated a French prose political allegory, which he assigned to the narrator of the Canterbury pilgrimage as a second attempt to tell an acceptable tale. His late translation of Pope Innocent's *Contempt of the World* or *The Wretched Condition of Mankind* is lost. As *The Parson's Tale* on the pilgrimage, designed to be the last, he combined in translation a Latin treatise on the capital sins and a penitential manual.

The first poetic expression of Chaucer's concern with moral issues is a relatively short poem, called *The Parlement of Foules*, 'The Assembly of Birds', after one of its three parts. Then follow the works for which he is famous, *Troilus and Criseyde*, and the unfinished *Canterbury Tales*, a collection of stories contained within a prologue and an epilogue, designed to be held together dramatically in an account of a pilgrimage from London to Becket's shrine in Canterbury Cathedral.

The order of composition of these works can be fairly

confidently determined from various indications. It is likely that the *Parlement* was written not long after 1380 and that *Troilus* was finished by 1389. As for *The Canterbury Tales*, the conception of the scheme of a pilgrimage as a framework for his narratives, and the realization of this as far as it went, belong to the last dozen years of Chaucer's life, but some of the stories it comprises were undoubtedly written earlier. It was between the *Parlement* and *Troilus* that he translated Boethius.

The *Parlement*, Chaucer's first perfected mature work, is a study of instinct and moral values, a commendation of disinterested public service, a devaluation of self-indulgent physical gratification, and an affirmation of the excellence of socially regulated natural behaviour. The opening of the poem, which is a dream-vision, suggests that the love is *fine amour*, but the development quickly corrects that suggestion.

'Love' was a polysemous word in Chaucer's English. In court poetry its first meaning would be *fine amour*, literary ritualization of libido, the personification of this in the god of love and his cult. It could also mean sexual desire, or affection between friends regardless of sex, or unselfish emotional attachment between sexual partners. In a philosophical context it denoted the Platonic principle which, in the language of Chaucer's translation of Boethius, 'governeth erthe and see, and hath also commandement to the hevene' (340). In the Christian Platonism of the twelfth-century Alain de Lille it signified the generative principle which ensures the continuation of the living world. As a religious term it signified the selflessness enjoined in the Great Commandment, or divine benevolence or the absolute idea of God. All those meanings were linked by connotation and implicated in one another in Chaucer's subconscious mind.

The *Parlement* successively considers three of them. In the third consideration, from which emerges a commendation of regulated and formally sanctioned control, there seems to be topical reference to royal marriage negotiations in 1380. If that appearance is correct the poem acquires the character of a mirror for princes, whether intended for the boy King Richard, just turned thirteen, or for his guardians and preceptors.

The first love considered is that which expresses itself in unselfish concern and service for others, implying self-regulation, detachment and philosophical perspective. The consideration takes the form of the dreamer telling of reading, before he fell asleep, in an old tattered book, 'Tullius on the Dream of Scipio', that is, the part of Cicero's *Republic* preserved in Macrobius's commentary on dreams. He reads how the first Scipio Africanus, Hannibal's conqueror, appears to a namesake grandson in sleep and teaches him. A true sense of values depends on understanding that men's intelligences, their souls, are immortal, their time in the world is 'a kind of death', the world itself a trivial element in the cosmos, and all man's achievement destined to ultimate oblivion. But man need not remain earthbound. Escape, fulfilment, lie in the exercise of the mind for 'commune profit', the public good. Reward for a life devoted virtuously to that end is translation to everlasting happiness. By contrast the souls of those who in self-indulgence have disregarded the natural and divine laws are bound to the earth in torment for many ages before their release and admission to happiness (310–11).

The second consideration, of sensual love, is carried out by allegorical personification and symbolic iconography. We are now in the dream, where the guide turns out to be that same elder Scipio of whom the dreamer was reading. He brings the dreamer into a walled park where, he says, there will be things to write about, 'if you had any aptitude'. Within the park, of which the dreamer praises the fresh beauty, he comes to a garden that is an earthly paradise: it has every pleasure of the sense—fragrance, music, soft airs; night never falls there; no man can sicken or grow old. What follows in that setting is, however, reductive. First the dreamer sees 'Cupide oure lord', the god of love, forging and filing arrowheads; his daughter Wilfulness tempers and finishes them for killing or merely grievous injury. There also are Sensuality, Skilful Procuring, Beauty Unadorned, Folly, Flattery, Intrigue and Bribe—in fact, a crowd of such. There is a temple; within it Priapus the phallic god stands in the place of honour 'with his sceptre in his hand'; men are setting garlands on his head. And in a secret corner Venus lies on a bed of gold; with her is Wealth who controls access to her. Venus is naked to the waist, her only garment a kerchief of the finest fabric. 'I liked the way she was covered,' says the dreamer with a verbal leer. Two young folk on their knees are crying for her help. 'But thus I let her lie.' Deeper in the temple is a wall hung with trophies, bows broken by maidens in scorn of Diana the chaste huntress. On the facing wall are frescos of lovers from the ancient past, Troilus among them, with the stories of 'all their loves and in what plight they died', from the names stories of disastrous loves characterized by abduction, seduction and desertion, self-destructive obsession, lifelong adultery, necromancy, broken sacramental vows, sacrilege, sexual tyranny, homosexuality and incest (311–13).

Even in the fantasy world where no one sickens or

grows old sexual indulgence appears unadmirable, its ludicrous aspect shown in the situation of Priapus, interrupted at the point of sexual assault on a sleeping nymph by the braying of an ass. The Venus who stands for luxurious sexual gratification answers to the furtive or the salacious or the heartless in human personality. And see how her service can bring unhappiness, says the unmistakably exemplary list of lovers. In the words of the 'old tattered book' of Scipio which the dreamer read so assiduously, they instance 'those who have surrendered to the pleasures of the body and have become, so to speak, its slaves, who in response to sensual passion have flouted the laws of gods and men' (311, 312).

This consideration ends dismissively; after the list of names Chaucer does not even make the dreamer mention that he left the garden of sensuous delight but turns him abruptly to his next function: 'When I had come back to that refreshing place I spoke of earlier . . .'

The last love considered is the sexual instinct in its right use, the force divinely implanted in creatures to ensure the continuation of species, where appetite is not self-indulgent but subjected to a design of life. It takes the dramatic form of an assembly, on Saint Valentine's day, of all birds except the solitary phoenix—'So many that there was hardly room for me to stand'—come together to choose their mates. The consideration acquires a philosophical dimension from the presence of Nature, successively called queen, empress and goddess, who presides over the assembly. Chaucer found her in the twelfth-century Latin poem deploring homosexuality called *Nature's Lament* by Alain de Lille, to whom with unexpected erudition the dreamer once refers. She personifies Greek *physis*, 'nature, essence, inborn quality', transcendentally the life-principle that informs the natural world. In Alain's poem she is God's viceregent, controlling the operation of the universe and the generative processes of the living world. In the *Parlement*, immeasurably more beautiful than any creature, she sits in presidency, in a clearing of the forest on a hill of flowers. On her wrist is a female eagle, her most perfect and greatly cherished work.

The birds sit by rank with the raptors, as the noblest, in the highest places. First among them is a royal eagle, and with him other eagles of lesser descent. These must choose first. They proclaim their choice in elegant ritual language. The royal eagle asks for the female on Nature's wrist, begging her mercy and grace; no one can offer her more perfect love or devotion. A second eagle of lower rank bases his claim on having loved her longest. A third is less courteous, pressing for an early decision: 'People are waiting!' He claims to be her truest lover. They dispute and the day draws to a close without a decision. The common birds are impatient to choose their mates, and Nature intervenes. The female eagle must make the choice herself, although Nature would recommend the royal eagle. The female begs for a year's respite, which is granted. Now the other birds are free to choose, and the joyful clamour of their song wakens the dreamer (314–18).

The courtship of the eagles has topical reference to the royal marriage negotiations between Richard's guardians and Wenzel of Bohemia, newly elected emperor, for the hand of his sister Anne. The royal eagle suggests Richard, the one who pleads longest service Friedrich of Meissen, to whom Anne had been betrothed by her late father seven years back, the impatient one the Dauphin Charles, whose suit was a last-minute French manœuvre to block the alliance between England and Bohemia.

Even the impatience of the common birds mirrors popular feeling that a wife should be found for the young king. There is an astronomical reference in the poem that has recently been shown to fit 1380, the year of the marriage negotiations.

The topicality, pretty enough in itself, ties the three parts of the poem together. The truisms that the highest fulfilment lies in unselfish service, and that the fantasy of unchecked self-indulgence in an earthly paradise is destructive, are translated into immediate, therefore vital, considerations: the desirability of dedicated government, a regulated life, a stable dynasty and strong alliances.

The *Parlement* instances Chaucer's attainment of formal and technical maturity. It is shapely, the exuberance of *The House of Fame* now well under control. He has developed a new metre, a graceful and dignified stanza of seven five-stressed lines, to replace the 'lyght and lewed' four-stress couplet he had apologized for; the longer line lends itself better to complex statement such as will be a frequent feature of Chaucer's next, long poem, *Troilus and Criseyde*. His style has been schooled by the models of Dante and Boccaccio. His fluency now commands a variety of registers between the verbal opulence of renaissance rhetoric and the naturalism of the English comic style that he will himself soon perfect.

Chaucer's developing insight of how poetry might function as moral philosophy can be seen in the *Parlement*, where he demonstrates relative values by juxtaposition and implication. Each of the three parts is meaningful in terms of the other two, but the meaning is never made explicit in the manner of the homilist. Simply by his mode of presentation he imposes on his reader an act of discernment corresponding to the act of choice by which a good or bad course of action is adopted. When, presently, Chaucer came to study behaviour in dramatic narrative, that understanding enabled him to develop a poetic, a theoretical and practical conception of his art, in which the issue of moral values and the act of choice, along with the factors which determine this, are a part of the fabric of the narrative, implicit and structural, not explicit and superimposed.

The *Parlement* also registers intellectual restiveness in its very nature as an examination of the human condition without recourse to canonical morality, specifically in its pointed representation of a pagan teaching the immortality of the soul and reward and punishment according to works. The doctrinal explanation of such a phenomenon was that the pagan had received an extraordinary grace that enabled him to anticipate the teaching of Christ or his Church. In terms of that explanation it might seem anomalous that the idea of a due reward for works fell foul of the belief in divine election held by at least one of the great Fathers of the Church, Augustine, or that this same pagan, notwithstanding the very special vouchsafement of grace to him, should also have conceived the notion of the ultimate forgiveness of wrongdoers, the heresy of universalism. Beneath these indications, expressed in the imperceptive dreamer's account of Scipio's vision, lies what Chaucer actually read in Cicero's text. His poem reads simply, at the equivalent point, 'Know thyself immortal'. That is an extreme redaction of a very heady statement.

Know therefore that you are a god, if in fact that is a god which quickens, feels, remembers, foresees, and which in a similar way rules, restrains and impels the body in its charge as the supreme deity controls the universe, and as the eternal god governs a universe that is in part perishable, so an immortal spirit governs your destructible body.

Chaucer had reached a point where his two preoccupations, writing, that is, the arrangement of language in patterns physically, emotionally and intellectually satisfying, and philosophical reflection, were becoming indistinguishable. What he now undertook, the translation of Boethius's *Consolation of Philosophy*, completed the process. It represented a sustained engagement with both the denotations and the resonances of abstract vocabulary in three languages, the Latin of Boethius, highly sophisticated notwithstanding its 'post-classical' date, the French of a translation ascribed to Jean de Meun which Chaucer consulted, and his own English.

The conceptual range and complex argument of the *Consolation*, which draws on Platonic, Aristotelian and Stoic thinking, topped up with the Christianized Neoplatonism of Augustine, evidently taxed that English most severely. The often laboured prose of Chaucer's translation reflects his difficulties with both vocabulary and the intricacy of the Latin sentence structure. Prose is even more dependent than verse on models, and nothing like this had been attempted in English since the Conquest. But the subsequent gain was large. Chaucer's style, in both verse and prose, benefited from the extended discipline of the translation. And intellectually the reward for the effort was immense. The initial appeal of the *Consolation*, which had emboldened him to attempt translating it, became a lifelong attachment. Boethian forms of thought henceforward played a main part in Chaucer's organization of experience. The stupendous sweep of the Boethian imagination, the assertion of the value of human intelligence in the personification of Philosophy, and the authenticity of the occasion of composition, in prison and in danger of death, now in a sense belonged to him.

The length of this translation, more than forty thousand words, shows how large a part of Chaucer's life study and writing had become. By the terms of appointment of his Controllership he had to be always present at the wool quay, to write his own accounts, and carry out all pertinent duties in his own person. Even when he was seconded on missions abroad in 1377 and 1378 he needed formal licences for a temporary deputy. Two similar licences for four months in 1383 and one month in 1384 do not specify the grounds, which could have been personal. Those for a licence, in February 1385, to exercise his office by deputy for the remainder of his tenure were almost certainly so. The Controllership was now a sinecure and he had time to write. The leisure he must have wanted so badly became, ironically, enforced in December 1386 with his replacement. Chaucer was out of office until July 1389. His wife died in the second half of 1387, and in those years he watched the acquisition of power by the Lords Appellant and Commons, the collapse of the court party, the judicial murder of his close associates Brembre and Sir Simon Burley, and the purge of an administration where he had many friends. It is tempting to speculate that the work of translation served to console him for at least some of that bad time.

4 Master craftsman into philosopher

Chaucer's next work, his greatest completed achievement, unmatched by anyone between Dante and Shakespeare, is *Troilus and Criseyde*, which he called 'The Book of Troilus'. It can be read as a deeply sympathetic study of a pair of star-crossed lovers. It is also an intensely serious examination of obsession, conducted in Boethian terms, sexual attachment so extreme as to disturb the personality. It considers, by narrative representation, the injury done even without intent by unregulated libido, and it represents the limitation of sexual sublimation. The insight and understanding Chaucer exhibits in that study are amazingly transcendent of fourteenth-century canonical morality.

The relation between the sexual instinct and the quality of individual personality became one of the two principal concerns of Chaucer's mature work. It developed out of his early exercises as a court poet, initially as an attempt to discover sense and order among the various conflicting medieval attitudes to women, to which nothing in modern thinking corresponds. His education and reading had filled his head with a mixture of discrepant responses to the existence of the second sex. In clerical literature Eve was vilified as the source of all human ills and Mary venerated as the mother of the Redeemer. There were the contrasting positions of Ovid's cynical *Cures for Love* and his *Heroic Women*. There was the exaltation of women in the poetry of *fine amour* and the observed fact of their extreme vulnerability. 'It is reckoned a game, nowadays, in your world', says one idealized woman to the dreamer in the *Prologue* to *The Legend of Good Women* who has written Chaucer's works, 'for a man to see how many women he can disgrace by seduction' (494). The cynical part of the *Roman de la Rose* pronounced that because of the legal subordination of wives anything worth calling love was impossible between marriage partners, but anyone could see marriages where the emotional relationship was deep and steadfast. For the good Bishop Brinton, Richard's confessor, whom Chaucer certainly heard preach, God had given women angelic beauty so that they might the better, as temples of the Holy Spirit, display the gifts of grace, but in actuality, by unchastity, they became habitations of the devil.

Chaucer represents every gradation of that variety of attitudes to women in his poetry, but in ways that make clear his understanding of them as oversimplified and therefore exaggerated reflexes of the most complicated of human relationships. And he knows the reason why that is so: in a work that makes play with traditional medieval antifeminism he pointedly inserts the consideration that women figure badly in books because these were written by men. He understands that sexual partnerships are like other human relationships, notwithstanding the disturbing physical factor and its effects upon rational judgement. To keep such relationships in good order there must be concessions, give and take: never any domination or exploitation of advantage, but understanding and forbearance. 'Every one of us, tired or off-colour or drink taken, is going to say or do something wrong some time or other; censoriousness serves no good purpose', he wrote in *The Franklin's Tale* (136). The balance of sympathy in Chaucer's work as a whole favours women. His representations of masculine sexual selfishness and the misery it causes are numerous and cruel. The women in his stories most often fall short of the ideal by deceit, but with one single exception he represents them with some degree of compassion and understanding. Nevertheless there is no mistaking his insight that, whatever the differences between the sexes and the complications set up by these in their relationships, men and women are impelled by the same physical and acquisitive urges, which can affect their value as persons.

To Chaucer's development of this concern his personal circumstances are necessarily relevant, and must be considered even though the risk of anachronism in biographical projections at such distance is extreme. One class of speculation can be confidently dismissed. The profession of eight years' lovesickness that opens *The Book of the Duchess*, the unrequited service to the god of love to be rewarded in *The House of Fame*, the intimation of loss of taste for love in the *Parlement*— these have no more necessary autobiographical validity than do the obtuseness and lack of judgement of Chaucer's dreamers and narrators.

We do know that Chaucer was married by 1366 to Philippa, one of the two daughters of a Hainaulter, Sir Paon de Roet, then of the queen's household and later Guienne King of Arms serving with the Black Prince. She was at the time a lady-in-waiting to Queen Philippa, and presently, after her death, to the Princess Constance of Castile and Leon, Gaunt's second duchess. They had children: two sons survived and there may have been a daughter. From their serving in separate royal households after 1369, they were evidently often apart. There is no evidence how they got on. But the terms in which Gaunt, in 1374, conferred a life annuity on Geoffrey

Chaucer both for his good and acceptable service, 'and the good service our well beloved Philippa his wife has done to our most honoured lady and mother whose soul is with God and also to our well beloved consort the queen', and the mundane circumstance that Chaucer often collected his wife's annuity payments, suggest that their marriage was at least a working relationship.

We also know that in 1379 or 1380, when the records show Chaucer's wife in Lincolnshire with Constance, he was involved with a London townswoman, Cecily Champaigne, whose father had been a baker. The information comes from a Chancery enrolment in which she 'remits, releases, and on behalf of herself and her heirs in perpetuity absolutely quitclaims Geoffrey Chaucer of every sort of action concerning both her rape and any other possible kind of suit or case which she ever has or had or could have had from the beginning of this world to the present day'. The release is witnessed by three knights of the king's chamber, Sir William Beauchamp, chamberlain of the royal household, Sir William (later Lord) Neville, one of Richard's admirals, and Sir John Clanvowe, a member of a group in Richard's service called the Lollard knights, and by two city magnates, one of whom, Sir John Philipot, had been alderman several times, and Lord Mayor in the previous year.

In the Latin *de raptu meo*, translated above 'concerning my rape', the noun can mean either 'abduction' as when Chaucer's great-aunt carried off his father, or unprovoked sexual assault in the modern sense of 'rape'. Almost as much ink has been spent on this record as on Sir Thomas Malory's record of imprisonment for crimes of violence. To judge by Cecily's father's will, which left her only twenty shillings in money and no land, she was not an heiress worth abducting. As to Chaucer having sexually assaulted her, two circumstances make that seem unlikely. One is the standing of the witnesses to the release, evidently intended to imply that there was nothing to hide, nothing deeply discreditable in question. The second is that, from evidence of entries in the Court of Mayor and Aldermen of London, two men, London citizens, one in debt to Cecily, were involved, not as her guardians bringing a charge on her behalf but in some legally sensitive way. There seems an obvious explanation: whether or not Chaucer had an affair with Cecily, these men had conspired with her or brought pressure on her to extort money from him by threatening a charge of rape, and Chaucer faced them down.

To balance that experience there was another side of Chaucer's world, compounded of a different class of anomalies, sometimes apparently governed by another set of rules.

It contained a number of women with remarkable personalities, whom he was able to observe and, up to a point, to know. These were not celebrities created by systematic publicity but exceptional people with characters remarkable enough to overcome the legal and social disadvantages of their sex. Edward's Queen Philippa was the first, whose sweetness of nature kept her five powerful and high-handed sons in a loyal familial affection exceptional in those times; yet she could successfully oppose the king at the height of his anger. By contrast there was Alice Perrers who, after Philippa died in 1369, got control of Edward and exploited his declining years. She was a flamboyant, rapacious, scheming woman, even ambitious for the husband she was cuckolding. Then Richard's mother Joan, Countess of Kent, widow of the Black Prince (her third husband), 'in her time', according to Froissart, 'the most beautiful woman in the kingdom and the most amorous', but also a wise guardian to her son the young king, and a resolute, often successful, peacemaker. There was Gaunt's first duchess, lovely Blanche, who never lost her place in his heart: his will, drawn nearly thirty years after her death, required his body to be laid beside hers, his 'very dear companion of former years'. There was young Richard's Queen Anne (they were married at fifteen) who kept him stable; for her Chaucer evidently had a special regard. And there was Gaunt's third duchess, Katherine Swynford, one of Blanche's ladies-in-waiting and the governess of her daughters. She became Gaunt's mistress in 1372, and in 1396, to legitimize their four children, he married her. She was Paon de Roet's other daughter, Chaucer's sister-in-law. Of her Froissart writes that she had a fine sense of protocol, which she will have needed.

John of Gaunt, whose life touched the lives of all these women, emotionally or politically or both, must have afforded Chaucer some means of organizing his impressions of them. The two men had known each other since 1357 and were subsequently both members of Edward's household. In 1369 Gaunt took Chaucer on campaign with him in France. Whether he asked for Chaucer or Chaucer volunteered, this implies esteem. When in 1372 Katherine Swynford became Gaunt's mistress and Philippa Chaucer one of the Duchess Constance's ladies, their lives became entangled in a relationship complicated further by their differences of rank. It seems to have continued in good order, extending beyond the lives of both to those of their children.

The emotion implied, however complex, cannot have blinded Chaucer to the huge anomalies in Gaunt's role as an actor in the play of human relationships. Gaunt made many enemies. He could be distant and unforthcoming in manner and was not undevious. By contrast he was a good landlord, handsome in giving and a man of ready clemency; he was loyal to both kings, strikingly so to Richard whose claim to the succession he could have contested on grounds of irregularities in Joan's first and second marriages. He was evidently a steadfast friend. He was a great patron of religion, pious in observances but lax in moral practice. In his relations with women there were corresponding anomalies. He got a daughter by one of his mother's ladies-in-waiting before he was twenty. His marriage with Blanche of Lancaster was arranged by his father for political reasons, to consolidate the monarchy by alliance with the greatest heiress in England. It turned into a love match. Almost three years to the day after Blanche's death he entered on his second marriage, dynastically ambitious and of his own devising. This time, within months, he took the mistress to whom he formed a lifelong attachment. He got four children by her, siring two lines of rivals for the throne. Without love he also gave his second duchess a pair, one of whom as Queen of Castile vicariously realized his ambition. He was a spectacular man to whom the rules might not seem to apply. As a study of the paradoxes of unregulated sexual gratification and deep sexual attachment, or of the politic balance of long liaisons and dynastic marriages, he afforded Chaucer an intimate, living instance of the complexity of rival considerations, animal, pragmatic, instinctively good or otherwise, some of the raw material of moral philosophy.

Not merely such personages, but their grand world, its formal elegance and grace, and leisure in everything but warfare, are mirrored in *Troilus and Criseyde*. The prince Troilus is second only to his brother Hector in prowess; Criseyde's father, albeit a defector, is a lord of great standing; Diomede, for whom she leaves Troilus, is the rightful claimant to a kingdom; even Pandarus is once summoned by the king and kept in attendance all day. Along with the matching setting there is a correspondence of emotional dimension and of extravagant action deriving from emotion.

The correspondence stops short in one particular. In Chaucer's actual Christian world not even the loves of princes were ultimately exempt from the strictures of the decalogue, whereas the Trojans had lived before the revelation of the perfect truth. That is a point Chaucer's public will not have missed, but he never makes it within the narrative. It is his design that within its limits the action is to be judged on its merits.

Chaucer's circle knew the names of Troilus and Diomede, and that they were rivals for the beautiful daughter of Calchas, from the presence of the triangle in a twelfth-century French verse history of the Trojan war. The story Chaucer tells follows in outline one which Boccaccio shaped at the suggestion of that triangle. His object in composing it was expressly to alleviate his own unhappiness at the absence of a woman he was in love with. He tells her in his preface how he had looked in old books for a man in a situation like his own. By telling that man's story he would keep himself distracted and so alive until her return—not that he had ever enjoyed happiness like that he was attributing to Troilo before Criseida was taken from him. He called his story *Il Filostrato*, in the mistaken notion that the name in Greek meant 'one stricken by love'.

In outline that story is a simple account of a love affair with an unhappy ending. Criseida's father Calcàs (in the *Iliad* a Greek soothsayer, here a Trojan) learns by divination that Troy will fall to the Greeks and defects to them, leaving his widowed daughter in Troy, innocent of complicity in his treason. Ettore grants her protection, and she withdraws into the retired life of a widow of means. But one day at a religious festival King Priamo's young son Troilo, till then undisturbed by love and a great scoffer at lovers, catches sight of her and is utterly smitten. He is at first without hope, but at length through the agency of his friend, her kinsman Pandaro, she becomes his mistress. They are happy until by the fortune of war the Greeks capture the Trojan knight Antenore, and Calcàs whom they esteem for his powers of divination persuades them to offer him in exchange for his daughter. Ettore opposes the exchange, but the Trojan parliament and Priamo decide upon it; Troilo can do or say nothing for fear of compromising Criseida and she will not run away with him. She is handed over, and helpless in the enemy camp, unable or afraid to steal back to Troy as she had promised Troilo, she accepts the Greek hero Diomede as lover. When Troilo learns this he sets out to kill Diomede in battle, but never succeeds and is at length cut down by Achille.

As Boccaccio tells that story it is about himself, an unembarrassed exposure of unfulfilled sexuality neither greatly moving nor particularly creditable to him. The part of the action which Boccaccio invented, in which Troilo becomes Creseida's lover, has the look of a sexual fantasy being displayed before the object of desire as a veiled proposition.

By contrast Chaucer's understanding of this story as essentially tragic was dispassionate and analytical, a penetration to its inherent meaning. His emotional involvement in it was complementary, the drive of the artist for creative achievement, for the gratifying sense of success. There was also the circumstance that he

was competing with Boccaccio. He too had been turning over old stories in his mind, in search not of one
that would express his 'secret and amorous sorrow', but
one that would lend itself to development in the terms
of a definition of tragedy he had found in a gloss in his
Boethius manuscript. His intuition of the aptness of this
story may even have been sharpened by revulsion from
the fulsomeness of Boccaccio's self-preoccupation, so
that he saw the rise and fall of Troilus's misfortune in
love in a perspective which brought out the dimension
of its essential pathos.

The measure of Chaucer's distance from the action is,
paradoxically, the degree to which he involves his reader
in the personages. It is as if these had not been brought to
life by him, but had asserted an independent existence.
So the emotional response of subsequent poets, Henryson
who in a continuation of the story visits the grisly
punishment of leprosy upon Criseyde for her inconstancy,
or Shakespeare, for whom she is a loose woman, is as
violent as if she had actually existed. Even modern
academics, who ought to know what Chaucer was
about, solemnly argue about Criseyde and Troilus and
Pandarus as if they had historical reality, even psycho-
analyse them. That is, of course, a triumph for Chaucer,
the one to which every writer of fiction aspires. But it is
only the beginning of his achievement in this work.

In the first instance Chaucer involves his audience by
making them participate in the realization of the
personages. These have to be filled out in the imagination.
Criseyde's beauty is angelic, but we have little detail of
it. Her height is average, her hair thick and wavy and
golden red, her fingers long and slender. Her eyes are
exceptionally lovely; but what colour? To visualize her
kneeling suppliant before Hector, or sitting with the two

ladies in the 'paved parlour of her house' (390, 402), it is necessary to finish her creation. So with Troilus. There are bold strokes: the arrogance of his emotional inexperience before he falls in love, the violence of his lovesickness, his inhumanly absolute constancy. How does he look to Criseyde from her window when, returning from a sortie, he rides past with his squadrons? His horse is wounded, his shield battered and studded with arrowheads, the helmet at his back damaged in twenty places. He is a more knightly sight than the god of war. The cheers of the people embarrass him (408). What were his features like? By the end of the story we have learned that he was taller than most, but well proportioned. As for Pandarus, he is only talk and restless movement and manœuvre. It is for the audience, the observers of the reported actions, to supply the light and shadows of personality in all three. Chaucer stands back.

The narrator of the story is correspondingly involved. He speaks in the first person, but it is wrong to call him 'Chaucer', for he is a fiction, as much a literary construct as the personages in the story he tells. Like them he is brought to being in the reader's consciousness by the historical Chaucer who organized the language of the text. The narrator speaks of himself as a translator, turning into English a Latin history of the siege of Troy by Lollius: the poet is rewriting and radically reinterpreting a near-contemporary Italian novella. The narrator in his role of translator disclaims responsibility for the events he reports; he is only following his 'authority'. The poet determines the events of the story, whether he adopts or adapts them from Boccaccio or invents them. The narrator sides with Criseyde against writers like his source, who criticize her inconstancy: the criticism is an invention. The narrator professes himself deficient in

75

the kind of sensibility needed for an adequately respon-
sive treatment of the subject: Chaucer's insight into it is
deep and searching.

The narrator exists as intermediary between the
personages in the written text, which also generates
him, and the reader. He becomes to the reader more than
simply a reporting voice, for he seems to acquire
personality by his response to the events he reports.
That response fluctuates: his insight is limited and
erratic, sometimes seems less good than that of the
informed and attentive reader. He is the first illustration
of the Chaucerian poetic which represents the human
condition from within, a model of the difficulty of
recalling the existence of moral issues, as, when at
length the lovers are in bed together, he exclaims,

> O blisful nyght, of hem so longe isought,
> How blithe unto hem bothe two thow weere!
> Why nad I swich oon with my soule ybought,
> Ye, or the leeste joie that was theere? (435)

> O night of bliss so long desired by them, what joy you
> gave to both! Why might I not have bought such a night
> with my soul, or even the smallest part of its ecstasy?

His function is referential, designed to recall the world
and values outside the room where the lovers are. Here,
by his regret that he did not sell his soul for such love, he
recalls them in an obliviousness of the outcome as ironic
as the lovers' ignorance of it. He is not Chaucer, but he
works for the poet, directing and shaping the reader's
responses and insights, either by inducing conformity
with his own or by provoking disagreement.

Chaucer exposes the action of his story to evaluation
in three systems: poetic, philosophical and Christian. It
is in the first of these that he makes particular use of the

narrator. The ethos of that system is *fine amour*, the poetic ritualization of courtship he had inherited from the French poets; this ostensibly governs the conduct of the personages. Its principles by Chaucer's time were, above all, the idealization of the lady and the abject subordination of the man. He had an obligation to love because being in love improved him. If by undeserved good fortune he was accepted as the lady's 'servant', his absolute duty was never to boast of his success, unfailingly to protect her good name, and to be totally constant. The question of the lady's constancy simply did not arise.

By applying that ethos to a love story in which the lady would prove inconstant Chaucer was unmistakably subjecting such idealization to scrutiny. His examination spans two descriptions of Criseyde. The first introduces her.

> So aungelik was hir natif beaute,
> That lik a thing inmortal semed she,
> As doth an hevenyssh perfit creature,
> That down were sent in scornynge of nature. (390)

The second is one element in a set piece of three, describing also Troilus and Diomede just before Criseyde, now in the Greek camp, is subjected to Diomede's formidable and favourably circumstanced technique of seduction.

> She sobre was, ek symple, and wys withal,
> The best ynorisshed ek that myghte be,
> And goodly of hire speche in general,
> Charitable, estatlich, lusty, and fre;
> Ne nevere mo ne lakked hire pite;
> Tendre-herted . . . (468)

Taken together those lines describe a paragon. 'She was

born with such beauty that she seemed something immortal, created to perfection in heaven and sent down to earth in scorn of what the natural world could create . . . She was temperate, straightforward, with good judgement in all matters, excellently brought up, gracious in speech to all, concerned for others, both dignified and vital, open-handed, unfailingly compassionate and sympathetic.'

The extravagance of the narrator's language in the first description, which represents her as a celestial rather than a natural and flawed creation, corresponds to Troilus's illusion, which survives until the anticlimactic discovery, shocking solely because of his obsession, that she is human and fallible. The reader is, however, prepared for that discovery; Chaucer has seen to this by making the narrator raise a number of seemingly gratuitous considerations that act to devalue Criseyde, not as a woman, but from extravagant idealization into womanhood. The narrator cannot say whether Criseyde had children; his books do not tell him, 'So,' he says, 'I drop the question' (391). When Troilus takes to his bed for lovesickness the narrator cannot say whether Criseyde did not learn of this or whether she was pretending ignorance: the story presently indicates that she knew nothing of Troilus's condition (394). Even before Criseyde realizes that she is in love with Troilus the narrator is excusing her in case some ill-disposed person might say, 'This was a sudden falling in love' (409). His source does not tell him whether she saw through, and therefore presumably acquiesced in, Pandarus's manœuvre that finally brought the lovers together (427). The narrator's book tells him that she really was sincere in her intention to come back to Troilus. Just as, when the lovers are first united, the narrator's forgetting not just the wretchedness to come but even his own need to be saved is a measure of the pitch of their ecstasy, so every such consideration sets the immediate event or occasion in a perspective of the disaster at the end. And there is thus no surprise at the closing detail of the second description, 'slydynge of corage' (at heart unstable).

As for Troilus, what most particularly commends him in the ethos of *fine amour* is his great constancy. That is a quality of which Chaucer recognizes the absolute value. In his epilogue he confers on Troilus, as if in reward for it, insight after death into the nature of illusion and of ultimate values. But Troilus is also there shown that his constancy was misdirected, related to his 'blynde lust' (479), 'blind passion'. And Chaucer takes pains to represent his behaviour as extreme in other respects. The king's son, terror of the Greeks, kneels to Pandarus in a prayer of gratitude for undertaking to plead his suit (400). He swoons when Pandarus finally gets him to Criseyde's bedside (432). When the decision to exchange her is taken he shuts himself in his room, rushes about it roaring in rage like a wounded bull, beats his breast violently, knocks his head against the wall, throws himself to the floor, dissolves in tears, is speechless with sobbing (443). Chaucer's language did not have terms like 'hysteric' or 'infantilist', but he was evidently familiar with the characteristic behaviour. Here the narrator's function is to ensure that the contrast between Troilus's prowess in battle and his inability to regulate his emotions should not be missed by repeatedly insisting on the former. The ideally submissive and constant lover of *fine amour* comes to appear a *reductio ad absurdum* of the cult and its conventions by his inability to cope with circumstances.

With Pandarus the exposure of the story to the ethos

of *fine amour* becomes an exposure of that ethos to condemnation. In plain terms, Chaucer represents him as seducing Criseyde for Troilus. He systematically reduces her, at the outset emotionally secure and serene, to the point of susceptibility and then manœuvres her into a situation where it is virtually impossible for her not to become Troilus's mistress. Because of torrential rain she is benighted while dining at her uncle's house. Only when she has retired to bed does he tell her that Troilus is there too. Pandarus importunes her to let Troilus come to her, and will not take no for an answer. If she wanted to resist there might be an outcry, and her women in a room nearby would wake, and there would be scandal. She does not know what to do or what she wants, is at her wit's end. She will do as her uncle advises (429–31). In *fine amour* convention Pandarus, as the third party in the love affair, coresponds to the friend or confidant of medieval romance to whom the lover can 'unfold his sorrows, pour out his heart'. But there is no medieval romance where friendship is carried to such length as this. Chaucer carefully excludes the possibility that Pandarus's role might be thought conventional. He has, evidently, been Troilus's friend from childhood; they grew up together: 'Whatever people may say, and whatever scrapes we were in, I have been your devoted friend all my life, and so shall be' (396). That does not describe a conventional relation. And he is also Criseyde's uncle, since her father's defection the man of the family responsible for her. Boccaccio's Criseida and Pandaro were cousins. From Chaucer's having changed their relationship it is clear that he meant Pandarus to be something else than a conventional figure from *fine amour*, a conveniently available device.

Pandarus knows his responsibility as Criseyde's uncle.

Even while he is working on her he says,

> 'me were levere thow and I and he
> Were hanged, than I sholde ben his baude,
> As heigh as men myghte on us alle ysee!
> I am thyn em; the shame were to me,
> As wel as the, if that I sholde assente,
> Thorugh myn abet, that he thyn honour shente.'
> (405)

'I would rather have the three of us hanged for a public spectacle than that I should be his bawd. I am your uncle. I too would be disgraced, along with you, if through my urging I were to be a party to his damaging your good name.'

And when he enjoins secrecy on Troilus, he says, 'I would never do this again for anyone, no matter how close to me. For you I have become, half in fun, half seriously, one of those who make women come to men—I don't say the name, but you know.'

> 'And were it wist that I, thorugh myn engyn,
> Hadde in my nece yput this fantasie,
> To doon thi lust and holly to ben thyn,
> Whi, al the world upon it wolde crie,
> And seyn that I the werste trecherie
> Dide in this cas, that evere was bigonne.' (424)

'And if it were known that I, by my contrivance, had put this deluded notion of giving in to your desire and becoming your mistress in my niece's mind, why, the whole world would cry out upon it and say that in this I had committed the worst betrayal ever undertaken.'

Pandarus's excuse is that he did it entirely for love of Troilus and not for money. Chaucer leaves the reader to judge how true that may be; the thought might cross his mind that treason runs in the family. By this point in the story Pandarus has lied repeatedly, always without comment from the narrator. There is one episode, Chaucer's invention, that suggests other less creditable reasons than affection for Troilus behind his discreditable behaviour. The language in which the episode is reported is pointedly ambiguous. The morning after Troilus and Criseyde have, by Pandarus's contrivance, become lovers in his house, he comes to where Criseyde is still in bed, alone. 'How are things this fine morning?', he asks. 'Do you know how to manage now?' Chaucer leaves us in doubt about what he does after that, but suggestively. And the narrator makes his one leading comment about Pandarus, 'I passe al that which chargeth nought to seye' (438), 'I leave out all that which it is unimportant to relate'. In the opaqueness of that situation the sublimations of *fine amour* dissolve.

Chaucer gave Pandarus many engaging qualities. He is full of good advice, good sense. It is foolish of Troilus to mope for lovesickness when he does not even know his chances of success. Let him tell Pandarus the woman's name and they can think about tactics. Criseyde should consider that she is not getting any younger. Why does Troilus not carry her off instead of letting her be sent to the Greeks? Pandarus and his kin will give their lives to help if need be. She will never come back to Troy; forget her, the town is full of beautiful women. Pandarus seems a real friend, ready with sympathy, obliging, ingenious and witty. The princes and Helen think well of him. Until closely scrutinized he seems highly plausible; then his personality proves to have no centre. He exists as a succession of entirely expeditious responses to situations. Whatever observation may underlie Chaucer's creation of him, in the story he serves a diagrammatic function, to illustrate the nature of action governed altogether by expediency, practical advantage, without regard to principle. And he speaks his own commentary on the consequences of such action, by describing to Troilus what must not happen: 'she forlost and thow right nought ywonne' (424), Criseyde ruined and Troilus in no way the gainer.

Fine amour has actually injured the lovers. It contains no element of the principle of moderation for its own sake, that rational control of impulse which might have safeguarded Troilus against his obsession; in fact Chaucer shows him as if encouraged by the cult. The only control it is seen to involve is secrecy, necessary for the successful pursuit of intrigues. But that control was what made it impossible for Troilus to oppose the exchange of Criseyde. Nor did *fine amour* protect her; rather it provided Diomede with the language and postures for her second seduction.

The conclusion of the examination is that sublimation does nothing to change the essential character of unregulated appetite, which would be better subjected to rational control than sentimentalized. The elegant language and attitudes presumed to refine or spirtualize libido appear ineffectual in a naturalistic representation, especially with the narrator as well-meaning but clumsy commentator. The seamy underside of the supposedly higher is exposed. In the words of one of the Canterbury pilgrims, the Manciple, who calls himself a plain, blunt man, the sublimation of *fine amour* is a sham.

> 'Ther nys no difference, trewely,
> Bitwixe a wyf that is of heigh degree,
> If of hir body dishonest she bee,
> And a povre wenche, oother than this—

If it so be they werke bothe amys—
But that the gentile, in estaat above,
She shal be cleped his lady, as in love;
And for that oother is a povre womman,
She shal be cleped his wenche or his lemman.
And, God it woot, myn owene deere brother,
Men leyn that oon as lowe as lith that oother.' (226)

'There is no difference, believe me, between a woman of high social standing, if she is unchaste, and a poor, common girl other than this—supposing they both behave badly—that the gentlewoman, the socially higher one, is bound to be called the man's "lady" and the other, because she is a poor woman, will certainly be called his "wench" or his mistress. And believe me like a brother, the first is laid as low as the second.'

Compared with the violence of Chaucer's reduction of *fine amour* as an evaluative system, his exposure of the story to philosophical examination is gentle. Different cultural experiences underlie the two processes. His rebellion against the modes of French court culture was an emotional experience, as it were a public contest, his independence hazardously won. It left him with a lack of respect for their principal exponent, Machaut. Chaucer is still, in *Troilus*, adopting postures of differentiation from that poet. By contrast his assimilation of the Boethian thinking that pervades *Troilus*, albeit strenuous, was uncompetitive, private and intellectual, its main emotional component a sense of enlargement. Moreover the conclusion the philosophical examination would reach was foregone, the steps to it familiar in another form.

The philosophical examination supplies, precisely for that reason, the intellectual shape of the poem. It centres on the main Stoic element of the *Consolation*, the teaching that a man renders himself proof against misfortune by detachment. In terms of that teaching Troilus is so utterly bound by attachment that misfortune has the power not merely to make him utterly wretched but to destroy him.

Chaucer shows a part of that process of destruction to be the clouding of Troilus's mind. According to contemporary psychological theory a man's faculty of understanding, his 'reasonable soul', functioned effectively according to the degree of its freedom from physical bondage. Everlasting and incorruptible, it could nevertheless, while in the body, be affected. The more it was immersed in the body, 'by likinge of fleisch other loue of worldlich catel' (by physical appetite or attachment to material wealth), the more sluggish and less perfect its understanding, the quality of its existence. So Troilus, when he is to lose Criseyde, conceives of himself as the victim of a malignant force personified as Fortune which raises men to peaks of happiness and success for the express purpose of casting them down in the instant when they fancy themselves most secure. Troilus even presumes to attempt the question of foreknowledge and freedom of choice: Chaucer puts into his mouth a fallacious argument set up in the *Consolation* by Boethius for Lady Philosophy to destroy. He decays into self-pity. His despair and efforts to commit battle-suicide after he accepts that Criseyde has left him and he has failed to kill Diomede complete the process of his destruction by excessive attachment.

The third evaluation was spiritual and Christian. Doctrinally speaking, what destroyed Troilus was not excessive attachment in itself, but attachment to the wrong object, to the false good. That would have been apparent to Chaucer's public. From their point of view interest would lie in his manner of proceeding. This was governed by a method of representation developed as he wrote this poem. Crudely described it has two features. One is to project or appear to project the narrative from a viewpoint within the action, here achieved by involving the narrator who would, we recall, have sold his soul for a night like Troilus's first with Criseyde. This heightens moral interest by implying that although the moral issues involved in the action may in the abstract be clear-cut and simple, the situations where they have to be discerned or acted upon are more often complex, discernment and application accordingly difficult. The second is to develop style as a moral index. So in this text of a story set in pagan times Chaucer inserts language that in moments of relevance calls to mind Christian liturgy or Scripture or doctrine.

The narrator's prayer for lovers in the prologue unmistakably recalls the bidding prayer that came before the sermon at mass. Troilus, entrusting Pandarus with the courtship of Criseyde on his behalf, echoes the prayer *In manus tuas*, 'Into thy hands, O Lord, I commend my spirit.' When he becomes Criseyde's 'servant', the language of his submission recalls a line from the Psalms, 'Thy rod and thy staff shall comfort me,' interpreted in the Middle Ages to mean that God afflicts those he loves (*Quem Deus diligit castigat*). Finally in bed with Criseyde, in a prayer of praise to the god of love he invokes him in Christian terms, 'O Charity!' That same prayer goes on to echo unmistakably Dante's hymn to the Virgin Mary in the last canto of the *Paradiso*:

> Qual vuol grazia e a te non ricorre,
> Sua disianza vuol volar sanz ali

'Whoso wol grace, and list the nought honouren,
Lo, his desir wol fle withouten wynges.' (434)

'If anyone desires divine grace and does not turn to you'
[Dante]/'If anyone wants a woman's favour and will not
respect your power' [Chaucer]—'his desire is like wanting
to fly without wings.'

Troilus sees Criseyde's acceptance of him as a lover in
terms of the doctrines of mercy and grace. She, respond-
ing, echoes Dante's *Nella sua volontade e nostra pace.*
Such echoes, very likely recognized, but certainly sub-
liminally felt by Chaucer's audience, would recall the
otherwise excluded world outside the boundaries of the
story, and its transcending values. They would prepare
for the extension from philosophical understanding of
the action to the Christian, doctrinal one. So Chaucer's
epilogue, where he silences the narrator and speaks in
his own voice, reordering love from creature to Creator
and Redeemer, who will not deceive, would come as no
surprise.

The use of narrative to particularize moral generaliz-
ations was no novelty. It was a commonplace of
medieval education that significance beyond the literal
was inherent in any story, and that this could, indeed
should, be extracted and generalized for moral edifi-
cation. There were collections of stories put together for
the use of preachers to that end. But such stories were
undeveloped, formulaic, and tendentious. By comparison
Troilus and Criseyde, as an extended study of human
and transcendental values conducted without pulpit
direction, was radically innovative.

What was wholly unprecedented was its excellence in
all its aspects as a literary work of art: the magnitude of
its conception as the sustained close examination of

three people entangled in a single set of events; its brilliance of formal execution in every particular from the organization of the parts down to the smallest detail of style; the dramatic immediacy of the personages; above all, the shaping of the action into a moving relation of the moral generalization to the human predicament. For this Chaucer had no model in any language. Whether by invention or adaptation, he had to establish his own system of forms and conventions to realize his own conception of the story, and to establish registers of style for effects not yet attempted in English.

Chaucer's initial stroke of genius was his perception of the treatment appropriate to Boccaccio's story, to conceive of and develop it as a 'tragedy', which is what he calls it. For this again he had no English models, no stage-plays to learn from, only a school definition in a gloss to his manuscript to Boethius: '*Tragedy* means an account of a condition of happiness and well-being that comes to an end in misery.' This gloss was evoked by, and designed to explain the concept of Fortune as a destructive agency by which the personages in the story account for their unhappy fate, but which was dismissed in the *Consolation*. Out of that inadequate definition and some formulaic illustrations Chaucer developed a literary kind. If, as is possible, he laid hands on any of Seneca's closet-tragedies, they will not have been much help.

At some time in the 1380s he was collecting stories of notable calamities. A number of his exercises in retelling them, relatively short and undeveloped, survive as the contribution of the deplorable Monk of *The Canterbury Tales*. From that assignment, and the reaction of some pilgrims, it appears that Chaucer thought little of them. But evidently when he came upon the story of

Troilus it commended itself to him as both answering to and transcending the definition: the account of the lovers' rise to the pitch of happiness would make the structure shapely, as well as developing sympathy for them and intensifying the poignancy of their separation. In all but the projection for stage performance his representation of their interaction is dramatic. It is even possible to see in the function of the narrator something like that of an Euripidean chorus.

In particular Chaucer identified the tragic dimension of the story as we understand tragedy, the particular quality of emotion which differentiates it from sensational catastrophe, in the actual obverse of the moral 'lesson' about values inherent in the story. For the susceptibility of Troilus raises the essential question of tragedy. If the gods are angry with a hero for his offence, why did they create him such a man as would commit it, or put him into a situation where he was bound to commit it? Why was Troilus susceptible to obsession? Why is Fortune hostile? In terms of such questions, which would continue to exercise him, Chaucer exposed his intelligent reader to tension between his critical detachment as a knowledgeable observer and the mounting sympathy of his engagement with the protagonists. Observing how the course of events creates and disappoints their expectation of happiness, and seeing their helplessness, that reader must experience compassion and dismay at the limitation of human ends and the vulnerability of mankind. Chaucer never directs him to any rigour of judgement. His epilogue dismisses paganism harshly, and reminds with power of the true object of love, but it does not judge Troilus or Criseyde.

5 The human tragicomedy

Chaucer emerged from the composition of *Troilus and Criseyde* as a major poet. He had established his subject, what Scipio in the *Parlement* had called 'mater of to wryte' (312), namely human behaviour, the human predicament as it appeared to his late fourteenth-century eyes. Without rejecting dogmatic Christianity he had discovered the intellectual gratification to be experienced through independent thought, specifically through assessing behaviour in lay and philosophical terms rather than those of canonical morality. And in his thus refined perception of the quality of behaviour he had sensed a correspondence between moral and aesthetic values. He had developed a poetic of dramatic narrative that represented experience from the point of view of personages within the action or of a narrator involved in this. He had acquired absolute command of language as an instrument for directing or controlling the response of reader or hearer. And he had a public trained to co-operate, keyed to the narrative personality in his poems.

The artistic compulsion that had carried him to this point, a drive to participate in literature as a creator—a 'maker', he would have said—and to measure himself in terms of his achievement, was intensified by his success with *Troilus and Criseyde*. In its epilogue he prayed, literally, for the grace somehow to write comedy. The landmarks of his growth to that point were the succession of poets whom he had undertaken, and successfully, to outdo: Machaut, the complacently subservient court poet, his imitator Froissart, Deschamps, in some respects a match for Chaucer but with no considerable work to his name, learned and pedantic Petrarch who had furnished a lyric for lovesick Troilus, Boccaccio. He knew himself in debt to each and a better poet than any of them. As to Dante, Chaucer accepted that he was temperamentally incapable of competing with a poem as egotistic as the *Commedia*; he would experiment with another concept of comedy radically differentiated from Dante's kind first by the self-effacement of its poet, and second by the absence of judgement and condemnation like that with which Dante had peopled his *Inferno*.

Chaucer's impulse was toward understanding rather than judgement, and his concern was with the predicament of the inhabitants of his immediate world rather than the damned and the saved of history. The shape in which his subject increasingly presented itself to him was determined by the eschatological crisis of medieval Christianity. This had taken a particularly acute form in the England of his time. At the centre of the crisis was the doctrine of original sin, implicit in the question why men behaved so badly to their Creator, refusing his abundant grace and persisting in wickedness.

Canonical theology could offer little comfort. Its grimmest response was to correlate the evident badness of the world and the chilling Augustinian teaching of predestination: many are called but few are chosen. Even enlightened theologians like Wyclif, who had no patience with the complacency of the ecclesiastical establishment, accepted that description of the relation between man and God. Commonplace theology like that of Bishop Brinton accounted for the situation by the argument of theodicy: the times are bad because God is punishing men for their exceeding sinfulness. But that raised the question why men accordingly do not remove the cause, why they persist in sin and the refusal of grace. To this the doctrinal answer was that men are sinful because of their evil inheritance from Adam, the corrupted nature which God visited upon him and his descendants for his disobedience in Eden. There was the consolatory teaching that God's mercy surpasses all his works, but this was cruelly tempered by the doctrine that the grace of mercy would be extended only to those disposed to receive it. And most men were evidently, because of the effects of original sin, not so disposed.

A dry intelligence might extend this argument. It was by God's forbearance that Satan had been able to tempt Adam in the Garden, and thus that Adam had committed the original sin. Yet God in his omniscience knew that Adam would fall, with the consequent loss of immeasurably many souls. How then, having thus created man for his damnation, could God be infinitely just? Such thinking was canonically condemned as impious and utterly sinful. God's ways, ran the rebuke, are incomprehensible to man. His will be done. The wisdom of this world is folly with God. It may require a major effort of the historical imagination to realize the oppressiveness of that situation, which invoked the essentially unreasonable quality of religious dogma in evidence of the inadequacy of human reason, that is, asserted that the dogma was true because it was inaccessible to the intellect.

The situation could exist and persist because there was as yet no intelligent alternative to belief. The idea of a random universe was abhorrent. The world was manifestly full of evil, but the Manichaean dualism in which the principle of evil, Satan, was held to be coeternal and thus coequal with the principle of good, the Deity, was unacceptable to any philosophically trained intelligence of the fourteenth century, for which, by definition, good must be in all particulars superior to evil. Only Christianity afforded the concept of an ordered universe, of a will acting to an end. Its weakest point was the doctrine of eternal damnation. The amiable heresy of universal salvation was in men's minds. Chaucer pointedly recorded a pagan expression of it at the beginning of the *Parlement*. In *Piers Plowman* there is a moment of visionary hope when Langland makes Christ proclaim, in a dream of the redemption, that he will come at the end of time 'crowned with angels and have out of hell all men's souls'. But to question the doctrine of punishment for unending time in hell was to threaten the base of ecclesiastical power. 'Let no man delude himself', wrote Cardinal Lotario dei Segni, later Pope Innocent, in *The Wretched Condition of Mankind* which Chaucer had translated, 'by saying, "God will relent in the end; He will not be wrathful for ever." O foolish hope! O deceiving assumption!' That dismissal was, paradoxically, strengthened by the manifest wickedness of men in all walks of life and office; and the deep imprint of estates satire, where the wickedness was particularized minutely, intensified the sense of the badness of the times. Estates satire, moreover, did nothing to explain, only complained.

The eschatological crisis found a variety of literary expressions in England. One was the voluminous Latin and French moral verse of Chaucer's friend John Gower, fluently recasting and filling out estates satire formulae. Another was William Langland's *Piers Plowman* which, while maintaining an orthodox position with some agility, touched every sensitive nerve in the anatomy of canonical theology concerned with sin, grace and salvation. Chaucer's response was *The Canterbury Tales*.

The work is shaped by his two compulsions, to artistic fulfilment and to understanding the human condition. It is, correspondingly, as much an expression of Chaucer's relation to literature as an examination of behaviour. Whether by his design or not it both records extended experiment in specialized narrative and functions as an analytic representation of his understanding of the human condition. The two processes appear inseparable: just as unmistakably as Chaucer's art in *The Canterbury Tales* was morally orientated it was self-gratifying.

Even the scale on which Chaucer planned the work—thirty pilgrims to tell two stories each on the way to Canterbury and two on the return journey—implies self-assurance and an inordinate compulsion to write. Huge ingenuity went into the design. Where a modern author with a corresponding purpose would have a choice of genres Chaucer had to devise his own: in the 1380s not even the general concept of *fiction* as a self-validating literary kind with its own truth existed. To meet the question of truth of report Chaucer had already used the dream-vision and the 'history' professedly translated out of Latin. Now, while developing with evident pleasure the role of the narrator, he established a unique and completely novel set of conventions of reportage.

The *Prologue* to *The Canterbury Tales*, Chaucer's most familiar work, tells how that narrator, at a well-known Southwark inn, the Tabard, about to make the pilgrimage to Becket's shrine, fell in with a chance-formed group of people with the same objective. His descriptions of them are often very detailed, but natural-istically unorganized. An arrangement to lighten the journey by telling stories seems to develop spontaneously out of a convivial evening. On the actual journey there is by-play between the tales, and occasional reference to geographical points *en route*. It all could have happened. But Chaucer's audience has met that narrator with the ostensibly Chaucerian voice, and his insistence on his responsibility to report verbatim amounts to a further caution. What's more, everybody knows that someone telling a story in a cavalcade of thirty-one riders would not be audible to many of the party. Moreover, almost without exception the stories the pilgrims tell would be beyond their capacity to conceive or deliver. Anyway pilgrims are proverbially liars. Here there was effectively a set of conventions, that is, understood signals to the audience, about the kind of literary experience they might expect from *The Canterbury Tales*, effectively a legitimization of Chaucer's fiction. Since there was no intention to deceive the question of falsification did not arise: the truth to be found here would be of another order than historical. By this device, which was also designed to carry his main message, Chaucer licensed himself to experiment in almost every existing kind of fiction, romance and anti-romance, exemplary tale, saint's life, bawdy fabliau, mock-heroic beast fable, and parody.

When Chaucer, at the end of *Troilus*, prayed for the grace to write comedy he had little more information about the comic mode than that it was extremely differentiated from the tragic. But his prayer was answered, and variously, for many features or parts of *The Canterbury Tales* are comic, and in a variety of senses of that term. The *Prologue*, where the occasion and the pilgrims are reported, is exquisitely satirical comedy of manners. The Prioress gives herself the airs of a lady of the court, but her beautifully correct French has a Middlesex accent. The Squire wants to be thought so ardently in love that he cannot sleep at all, but his liveliness and

energy belie this. A philandering friar affects a slight
lisp, 'to make his English sweet upon his tongue'. The
wives of the city burgesses have their mantles 'roialliche
ybore', carried for them as if they were queens. The one
passion of a spiritually slothful monk is coursing hares
on horseback. The narrative links between tales are
accomplished burlesque or knockabout farce with a high
degree of dramatic development. Traditional hostilities
like those of miller and reeve (farm manager), or friar and
summoner (policeman of the ecclesiastical courts), are
exploited: the enemies score off each other by the stories
they tell. Here the Host of the Tabard, who came along
for the fun, is a prominent figure. He keeps the peace
with alternate diplomacy and blustering, mocks the
male clergy with country humour; his reactions to the
various tales are caricatures of simple or superficial or
half-comprehending response—except for his totally
accurate criticism of the narrator's attempt. All the
fabliaux, the bawdy tales, are consciously comic; several,
notably that told by the Miller, are comedies of reversals
of a shapeliness unsurpassed before Molière. *The Nun's
Priest's Tale*, the folk-story of the cock and the fox, is
sophisticated mock-heroic, an intrinsically comic mode.
Our hero the barnyard cock Chanticleer has a pre-
monitory dream that he will be caught and killed by a
beast 'like a dog' with, of course, the exact coloration of
a fox. His favourite hen, 'the beautiful young Lady
Pertelot', has no patience with him.

> 'by that God above,
> Now han ye lost myn herte and al my love.
> I kan nat love a coward, by my feith!
> For certes, what so any womman seith,
> We alle desiren, if it myghte bee,

To han housbondes hardy, wise, and free,
And secree, and no nygard, ne no fool,
Ne hym that is agast of every tool,
Ne noon avauntour, by that God above!
How dorste ye seyn, for shame, unto youre love
That any thyng myghte make yow aferd?
Have ye no mannes herte, and han a berd?' (200)

'God in heaven! Now you have quite lost my heart and
love. As truly as I have been faithful to you I do not know
how to love a coward. Be sure of this, whatever any
woman may tell you: all of us—if only it could be—want
to have brave husbands, wise and generous, and discreet
too, of course, not niggards or fools, certainly not
someone afraid of every edged weapon, no sexual boasters
either, I say again, by God! How could you dare admit to
the one you love that anything at all had the power to
strike fear into you? You with your beard! Don't you
have the courage of a grown man?'

The narrator's first attempt, the tale of Sir Topaz, is
totally assured parody of the bad romances. The function
of the narrator himself is comic, but always ironically.
His comedy is realized in the first instance whenever a
reader takes him for Chaucer; he is never so named in
the text, and another pilgrim speaks knowledgeably in
his presence about Chaucer as if the latter were not
there. The narrator's imperceptivity and bad judgement
are factors of meaning as were those of the dreamers and
the 'translator' of *Troilus*. He tells the Sir Topaz parody,
the only bad tale in the collection; after a few hundred
lines Chaucer has the Host check him abusively, and he
tries again with the only dull tale, a long-winded
political allegory that Chaucer had originally translated
from French as an exercise in writing prose.

97

Essentially comic personalities stand out in the *General Prologue* and the *Tales*. The most elaborately developed is the Wife (that is, woman) of Bath, who describes her life and exposes her character with totally credible volubility in a perfect dramatic monologue. She is an aggressive woman, and highly sexed. She has buried five husbands, the first three, in her words, good, rich and old. She led them the hell of a life, and they, by their successive deaths, left her comfortably off. The last two she calls young and bad. One deceived her and one beat her: these were the men she loved. Now she is getting on and her looks are going. 'Nevertheless, welcome the sixth!' And in the meanwhile,

> 'Lord Christ! whan that it remembreth me
> Upon my yowthe, and on my jolitee,
> It tikleth me aboute myn herte roote.
> Unto this day it dooth myn herte boote
> That I have had my world as in my tyme.
> But age, allas! that al wole envenyme,
> Hath me biraft my beautee and my pith.
> Lat go, farewel! the devel go therwith!
> The flour is goon, ther is namoore to telle:
> The bren, as I best kan, now moste I selle:
> But yet to be right myrie wol I fonde.' (80)

'Christ! When my youth comes into my mind, and what fun I had, it tickles the very roots of me. To this day my heart lifts to think how I have lived to the full in my time. But old age, with its way of poisoning everything, has taken my beauty and vigour away. Well, they're gone. Goodbye to them and the hell with it! The flour is finished—that's all there's to it—and only bran to peddle, as best I can. Just the same, I mean to keep cheerful.'

The ultimate scoundrels on the pilgrimage embody

the black comedy of totally corrupted personality: the Friar who sells the absolution of the sacrament of penance; the Summoner, a vicious, blackmailing police-man of the ecclesiastical courts; and the Pardoner, a cynically dishonest fund-raiser.

The dominant mode of *The Canterbury Tales* is, however, tragicomic, its prevailing theme the failure of men and women to realize an ideal. Even the actual pilgrimage symbolizes such failure, for the institution was designed as a deeply pious activity to be conducted with prayer and religious exercises, not an occasion of entertainment.

The apparently casual miscellany of pilgrims, the party 'of sondry folk by aventure yfallen in felawshipe', in the words of the *General Prologue* (17), conceals a process of selection. All come straight out of estates satire. They lay claim to life in our imagination as vividly conceived and credible personages by the detail of the narrator's report of them. They have a quality of portraiture absent from our impressions of Troilus and Criseyde, whom we know chiefly from their successive states of mind. The Canterbury pilgrims are triumphs of arrangement of language; a direct relation asserts itself between their appearance, dress, physiognomy and speech and their 'condicioun', as the narrator calls it, their character viewed in fourteenth-century moral terms. The imaginative reality of some is so particularized that it has been possible to argue plausibly, if not conclusively, that they represent historical persons of Chaucer's time. He does nothing to discourage such identification, indeed once reveals the trick of suggesting it, when one of his pilgrims, the Pardoner, describes how he preaches maliciously against his enemy.

> 'Though I telle noght his propre name,
> Men shal wel knowe that it is the same,
> By signes, and by othere circumstances.' (149)

> 'Even though I may not give his real name he will
> certainly be identified by distinguishing marks and other
> circumstantial details.'

But almost all the pilgrims are in fact constructed upon moral diagrams. They are dramatizations either of estates satire formulae that specified the typical shortcomings of those in the various lay and clerical offices and walks of life, or else of ideal figures the opposites of such formulae. Here Chaucer's art and moral concern are absolutely inseparable. Every detail of the narrator's reports by which these dramatizations are achieved and the illusion of the credible personage created represents an act of the poet's critical judgement in both the poetic and the moral sense.

Each pilgrim represents a complex of such acts of judgement. Of the Friar on the pilgrimage the narrator reports that he was well acquainted with innkeepers and barmaids—he knew the taverns in every town—but not with a single leper or beggar woman.

> For unto swich a worthy man as he
> Acorded nat, as by his facultee,
> To have with sike lazars aqueyntaunce. (19)

> For it was unbecoming to a man of such standing and
> ability as himself even to speak to diseased lepers.

The distance of that opinion from the intention of St Francis, who founded our Friar's order expressly for the charitable care of the lepers and the destitute, invites moral criticism. It does not need theology to appreciate the grossness of the anomaly. That the narrator seems unaware of this signals irony, and identifies the expressed opinion as the Friar's own; this forces an assessment of him on the reader. If the reader knows that Chaucer is here echoing the satirical representation of False-Seeming, Hypocrisy, in the *Roman de la Rose*, he will appreciate the depth of the irony the more. But Chaucer has not finished with the Friar.

> It is nat honest, it may nat avaunce,
> For to deelen with no swich poraille. (19)
>
> It is not appropriate; it can't get one anywhere to have to do with trash of that sort.

The shift to the present tense makes the reader hear the cynical tone of the Friar's actual voice. So the criticism of a total moral misdirection in the Friar's way of life is realized as a dramatic event. Morality and art are in full accord by the poet's exquisite contrivance.

Most of the pilgrims fall short of an ideal which emerges clearly from Chaucer's later poetry and comprises both absolute philosophical and Christian values. It is of a harmonious personality, inclined to right conduct, characterized by integrity, that is, truthfulness, uprightness. Theologically the ideal was last realized in the state of Adam before the Fall. Philosophically it should have been within the attainment of reasonable men, for it contained its own imperative: evil and sin, a deficiency of natural harmony, were not merely contrary to divine law but against reason. Good conduct was valuable in itself, without consideration of reward or punishment. It was aesthetically excellent. Those who fell short of it were inevitably in some respect unadmirable, ugly. The pathos of the human condition lay in the conflicts and confusions of values by which the ideal was rejected. Chaucer in *The Canterbury Tales* made literary capital of the effects of such rejection upon personality. The Summoner and the Pardoner are extreme cases which approach the grotesque. But he seldom altogether refused compassion. This sprang from the underlying consideration, why people are as they are. Why does mankind labour under the burden of sin?

Every age has its concerns, and those who live in it particularize these further. Notwithstanding the unfinished state of *The Canterbury Tales*—we have a prologue and twenty-four tales, one apparently meant to conclude the work—it is possible to identify from the direction of emphasis those anxieties of the times which particularly engaged Chaucer.

With a major one, the related issues of divine foreknowledge, predestination, future contingencies and free will, he had already involved himself in translating Boethius. The experience seems to have distanced that concern, as if showing him the aridity of epistemology, that it changes nothing except the terms of a problem. About the related issue of the value of works as a means of salvation he seems to have formed his own conclusions, expressed in literary representation of the intrinsic superiority and self-validating quality of virtuous conduct. Among the particular issues of corruption raised in estates satire one which evidently concerned him with great immediacy was the delinquency of clergy with care of souls, namely parsons who neglected to teach or mistaught their charges, and the friars who in the abuse of the sacrament of penance for financial advantage muddied the channels of God's grace to sinful man. How particular and reflective was this concern shows from his absolute command of the language of ecclesiastical reform. The good Parson of the pilgrimage, who tells the final tale designed to show the route of that glorious pilgrimage to the perfection of the heavenly Jerusalem, answers in every excellence of character and conduct, detail by minute detail, to estates criticism of ignorant and bad parish priests.

The question of Chaucer's attitude to one particular issue, the morality of warfare, is raised for modern readers by his account, in the *General Prologue*, of the campaigns of the 'verray, parfit, gentil' (18), that is, 'true, faultless, gentle', knight. By Chaucer's time canonical thinking about warfare had been forced into the awkward shape of a paradox. It was possible to conceive of a just war to resist or disarm unlawful violence or to right wrongs. But the fighting man sinned (this was a Wyclifite point) against charity with the first blow struck. The paradox was made acute by actuality: the territorial wars of the papacy were a scandal, and wars between Christian peoples were deplorable. Even the righteousness of warfare to recover the Holy Places or against the enemies of the faith was questioned, principally when it was not successful.

Chaucer's Knight served with distinction in the king's wars against the French. So did every able-bodied English gentleman of the time, including a group of knights in Richard's court with advanced Lollard views, one of whom actually wrote in condemnation of warfare. Chaucer reports that service in a short clause. Otherwise the Knight's earliest named campaign was the siege of Algeciras in 1343, the latest, cavalry raids in pagan Prussia and Lithuania in 1390–1. Between the two he campaigned in Turkey, Egypt, North Africa, and with the notable Castilian fleet. It is unlikely to be accidental that the list begins with a battle where Henry Duke of Lancaster, the Duchess Blanche's father, had fought, ends with one in which her son Henry of Derby took part, and comprises others where Henry's father-in-law the Earl of Hereford and Chaucer's friends the Scropes had fought. The span of those campaigns, from 1343 to 1390, is too large for one man's career. It looks paradigmatic, as if designed to sketch a tradition of which Henry Bolingbroke, Earl of Derby, was the newest representative. These men were not mercenaries, but adventurers living the tradition of knight errantry in a historical situation. They paid their own way, or in Henry's case his father Gaunt paid: the accounts survive. It is hard to see the description of Chaucer's Knight's dedication to 'Trouthe and honour, fredom and curteisie' (17), 'Integrity, self-respect, open-handedness and considerate behaviour', as ironic. The connotations of those terms in fourteenth-century English were absolutely favourable.

Chaucer's poetry registers his perception of the horrible face of war and the monstrosity of violent oppression. He had, after all, negotiated with John Hawkwood, the most notorious captain of mercenaries of his time, and Barnabo Visconti, the tyrant of Lombardy. He cannot have missed the argument that converting the heathen was more meritorious than killing him and was bound to accept it as undebatable. He will also have observed that this point was most often made not in criticism of the military class but as a rebuke to slothful clergy, notably to bishops whom the pope had appointed to episcopates in heathen lands, who called for crusades that would put them in possession of their exotic sees. Christianity was no doubt a religion of peace. Meanwhile there was recurrent, mounting Turkish pressure from the east. Already by 1371 the Ottomans were in the Balkans and Hungary. A new crusade to unite Christendom in its own defence was actually proposed in the early 1390s. The paradox came to rest in the actuality that violence is a fact of life; that since it cannot be suppressed it is best channelled; that the counsels of the Sermon on the Mount and of turning the other cheek are not of this world. Chaucer's Knight is actually an enlightened creation, not as a deeply ironic advocacy of non-violence but because he embodies the best compromise possible in his time between the ideals of a religion founded on charity and natural human aggressiveness.

The issues which most deeply concerned Chaucer, and about which he shows enlightenment beyond his times, have to do with a different sort of conflict in more pressing circumstances, namely that within the individual between instinctive urges and reasonable intelligence, between two sets of values, one immediate and variously sensible or accessible, the other absolute and transcendental. What distinguishes Chaucer's concern, beyond its depth, is the lay and philosophical terms in which he viewed the conflict and the quality of his literary representation of it. It is notable, also, in constituting an assertion of the validity of human intelligence as both a determinant and a criterion of human behaviour.

Chaucer was thinking and writing within the confines of what modern philosophers call a 'closed system', specifically a religion with dogmatically prescribed answers to fundamental questions. That system dismissed conflicts of values by invoking the transcendental quality of one value set: this was absolute and in fact no conflict existed. The superiority of the heavenly good to any earthly good was infinite. Chaucer's concern was specifically with the anomaly, forced upon his intelligence by observed experience, that the conflict which in doctrinal terms did not exist nevertheless appeared to persist, and with the effect of that anomaly upon people, personality.

The two forms of this conflict which most preoccupied Chaucer were shaped by the sexual and the acquisitive urge. *The Canterbury Tales* consist largely of studies of their effects upon people, how one or the other prevails over the reason which recommends good conduct, that is, the regulation of libido and the appetitive urge, both for its own sake and out of consideration for others.

Sexuality, masculine and feminine, appears in much of Chaucer's poetry but especially in the *Tales*, as the cause of fatuously unintelligent and wayward behaviour, or adventurism where sexual conquest becomes a sport, or as a means of dominance or punishment, or an instrument of financial advantage. In particular Chaucer represents the capacity of sexual selfishness, inconsiderate self-gratification, to cause unhappiness and do injury to others; the damage to personality, especially feminine, by the deceit implicit in sexual intrigue; how the need for this affects the person's sense of value. His studies vary in complexity and method. A simple case is Alison in *The Miller's Tale*, of all the women Chaucer created the most elaborately and enthusiastically described. What devalues her is not so much the deceit of her husband, who was too old to marry her in the first place, as the fact that it is she who thinks up the undebatably nasty trick to dispose of her unwanted second suitor. Lady May in *The Merchant's Tale*, whose adultery can seem similarly excusable, loses value by the outrageousness of her lies to her blind and besotted husband. At the very moment before she betrays him, and when he has just protested his love for her, she says,

'I have a soule for to kepe
As wel as ye, and also myn honour,
And of my wyfhod thilke tendre flour,
Which that I have assured in youre hond,
Whan that the preest to yow my body bond;
Wherfore I wole answere in this manere,
By the leve of yow, my lord so deere:
I prey to God that nevere dawe the day
That I ne sterve, as foule as womman may,
If evere I do unto my kyn that shame,
Or elles I empeyre so my name,
That I be fals; and if I do that lak,
Do strepe me and put me in a sak,
And in the nexte ryver do me drenche.
I am a gentil womman and no wenche.' (124)

'I have a soul to preserve in virtue just as you do, and my
chastity too, and the tender flower of my womanhood
that I committed to you when the priest made my body
bond to you. And by your leave, dear husband, I want to
say this: I pray to God that, if ever I disgrace my kin or
damage my good name because I am unfaithful to you, I
may not fail to die as ugly a death as a woman can. Have
me stripped and put in a sack and drowned in the nearest
river. I am a gentlewoman, not a common creature.'

Here the essential nature of dishonesty is communicated
by the discrepancy between the high flow of emotional
language and the actual situation. Style is an instrument
of moral judgement. In *The Shipman's Tale* a monk
borrows money from a woman's husband to buy a night
in bed with her. No one is obviously the worse for their
adultery. Here there is no such clear stylistic direction.
The manner of narration is pointedly non-committal. At
the end of the story no one appears the worse for what

has taken place. But the very absence of comment amounts to an invitation to consider whether a question of values arises in their situation.

As to the acquisitive instinct, Chaucer registers its effects on a gallery of frauds, cheats and scoundrels. The same criteria are applied here. What is the effect upon personality, and what injury does a particular dishonesty do? With respect to the first Chaucer creates imposing façades. A lawyer of the highest rank in the profession, immensely learned in both common and statute law, puts his learning to use not in the administration of justice but in acquiring landed property. A merchant of great presence and standing deals illegally in foreign currency and speculates on credit; if he were subjected to audit he would prove to be in debt. We are thus invited to consider the nature of sham. In another category, an uneducated manciple, the catering manager of an Inn of Court, can outwit the thirty and more learned lawyers who employ him. The narrator asks

> Now is nat that of God a ful fair grace
> That swich a lewed mannes wit shal pace
> The wisdom of an heep of lerned men? (22)

> Now, isn't that a very beautiful instance of divine favour, when the shrewdness of a man like that, who can't read or write, can best the wisdom of a heap of learned men!

He seems equally to admire the Reeve who has cared for the management of his lord's estate to such effect that he has money secretly put by, a lovely house on a hill in a grove of trees, and money left over from his peculation to lend the lord. The reader can share his relish. Lawyers, after all, are fair game, and a heedless spendthrift lord deserves to be cheated. But this does not abolish the dishonesty of Manciple and Reeve. The amusement is possible only because neither the learned benchers nor the extravagant lord will suffer from it. Here is a kind of gradation of immorality. In the representation of other sorts of dishonesty there is no such readily available mitigating circumstance. The charlatan Physician, well aware that his medicines against the plague are useless, nevertheless exploits the fear of it for his own profit. The worst dishonesty of all is that of the simoniacal Friar, the blackmailing Summoner, and the consummate con-man Pardoner, who prey on human weakness and the fear of damnation. The comedy they instance is a grotesque one of extreme distortion, not deliberate like that of great clowns, but unconsciously brought on by the falsity of their values. They are all in their way successes: we are made to see how their kinds of success render them deficient in integrity, which has been sacrificed to the immediate value of financial advantage and self-gratification.

All fall short of a Chaucerian ideal, the condition of the harmonious personality in which the reasonable soul exists most perfectly because not submerged in 'likynge of fleisch' (physical desire) or 'loue of worldly catel' (the acquisitive urge). Of course Chaucer recognized and represented other sources of disharmony, notably sloth and vanity. But the emphasis in both his pilgrim portraits and the tales is on the two primary urges as the main forces in the shaping of behaviour, on the variety of human forms that selfishness or deceitfulness prompted by one or another of them could take.

Canonical moral teaching applicable to every person or narrative situation Chaucer represented was available, and there is no indication that he was ignorant of, questioned, or rejected any of its positions. Indeed his *Parson's Tale* sets them out in elaborate detail. What does appear is that in the Canterbury *Prologue* and a number of the tales Chaucer elected to examine morality without reference to that teaching, as if with the intention of coming to its conclusions from an aesthetic and intellectual, not canonical position. The decision, in effect to ignore the closed system which contained him, put him in the position of moral philosopher and led him, by way of discovery of the distinction between judging actions from a moral standpoint and examining the nature of moral judgement, that is between ethics and meta-ethics, to the concept of value, expressed in personality and behaviour, as an intellectual absolute.

The decision was one to which both his times and his particular practical and cultural experience had moved him. Simply the restiveness of an intelligence oppressed by the anti-intellectualism of an intellectually undistinguished ecclesiastical establishment set him on the way. Then, moral philosophy was the only area in which an educated layman could move freely and confidently; it was also that one in which he had seen pagan philosophers, notably Cicero and Seneca, attain in their disadvantaged unenlightenment to intrinsically admirable concepts of value in behaviour. Strongest of all persuasions was the urge to use dramatic narrative, the literary kind he had perfected, as a vehicle of philosophizing not by disquisition but by poetic demonstration, by the vivid evocation of personalities and their representation in action.

By building into his personages the axiom that every sane person wants both to be the best kind of person and have the best kind of life he put them into moral focus, for that raised the question of their conception of bestness. In imputing success to them he raised the question of relative value systems: what clinched the success of the Friar, 'the beste beggere in his hous' (19), was to be able to extract money even from a destitute widow. In representing the same Friar's contempt for the principle of service to the destitute for which his order had been founded he showed that for a person to disregard a moral value, not to care about value, reduces his own value. In the detail of his representations there is the insight, possibly founded on Scipio's counsel, that in the scale of philosophical values self-gratification takes a lower place than any activity that benefits others; also that between self-gratifying activities there is gradation. Near the top is the gratification of certain classes of vanity, the Clerk's pride in his twenty volumes of Aristotle and Aristotelian commentary, the poet's own pride in his work; at the bottom callously selfish gratification of appetite, like Diomede's cool and calculated seduction of Criseyde, which destroys her (460–1, 468–9).

Not all Chaucer's narratives are readable as studies in moral philosophy. In some the morality is plainly Christian; in some, artistically self-indulgent, the morality is not evidently to the fore. But in others he sets up problems of absolute ethics. From *The Franklin's Tale* the question emerges whether a husband is ever right to advise his wife to be unfaithful to him, from the *Physician's*, whether in any conceivable situation it could be moral for a father to kill his daughter. The questions are not answered: a moral definition is required from without. Chaucer also makes narrative function speculatively. To do injury to others is axiomatically immoral: *The Shipman's Tale* examines the converse of the axiom, whether if no one appears to be injured by a set of actions any issue of morality is raised. Chaucer's procedure is to represent the action with obtrusively studied tonelessness, so that nothing comes between the reader and the telling detail of the events. In consequence what might have been a saucy fabliau acquires the appearance of a paradigm of the ugliness of deceit, the lying appearing more detestable than the adultery. The monk and the woman are represented as thinking that they have come off well. In holding that opinion they have lost value, and in their lack of concern about this incurred further loss. They have both, in fact, been injured.

Chaucer's speculative intellect penetrated to the deepest philosophical question of morality. Why should there be conflicts of values, a predicament of choice? If there are absolute grounds on which moral choices can be reasonably made, and no genuine dilemmas of choice exist, why do people choose wrongly? That question is the source of his great sympathy for the human predicament. In view of his religious conditioning it shows him amazingly perceptive.

That feature of the issue which ultimately most concerned him was not why people knowing the right choice make the wrong one, or why, if the difference between right and wrong is absolute, it should be difficult to identify the right choice. He understood very well the appeal of the false good, and let it show as if undimmed through the eyes of his personages confused in choice. What struck him was the question why some people should be able to make right choices easily, and in such a way that out of a succession of these they developed harmonious personalities, the quality of integrity, while others would knowingly make the wrong choice, or mistake the right choice, or not even realize that a choice existed. Ideally the capacity for right action would be inherent in any reasonable person, but the reality appeared most often otherwise. Whether the capacity for moral action was present in anyone had an accidental look. Here Chaucer anticipated the modern moral philosopher's concept of constitutive luck, that set of accidents by which a person has the qualities that enable him to conduct himself as a reasonably moral individual. The concept, implying randomness or confrontation of the doctrine of original sin, was theologically abhorrent, and reaching it Chaucer was brought up short by the confines of the closed system.

6 Conclusion

Like his poetry Chaucer's actual career has a quality of tragicomedy. It would be possible to draw two graphs of his life, a constantly mounting one of artistic capability, and a falling one of depression with the world in his time, what William James called weariness of the spirit, which included diminution of his own self-esteem. In his late works there is no evidence of cynicism, but unquestionably several of the lyrics he addresses to his friends register disappointment and bitterness. Some of this was certainly politically based. Here is his view in a balade (*Lak of Stedfastnesse*) formally addressed to Richard some time after 1389.

> Trouthe is put doun, resoun is holden fable;
> Vertu hath now no dominacioun;
> Pitee exyled, no man is merciable;
> Through covetyse is blent discrecioun. (537)

> Integrity is devalued, reason accounted idle talk; right conduct has lost its power as an effective ideal, compassion is in exile, no man shows mercy, discernment is blinded by covetousness.

Some of his depression may have originated simply in the expense of energy required to maintain some degree of confidence in himself and his world.

Presently Chaucer ceased to write. The incompleteness of *The Canterbury Tales* is an emblem of his admission of defeat. 'When I was young', he says in a lyric to his friend Scogan, 'I used to compete',

But al shal passe that men prose or ryme;
Take every man hys turn, as for his tyme. (539)

Whatever is written in prose or rhyme is bound to be
forgotten. Let every man make the most of his moment
of success while it lasts.

There was no way in which Chaucer could have
assessed his own achievement, or have had any inkling
of what a challenge his deeply perceptive and compassionate representation of the human predicament with
its complexity of moral choices was to the doctrine of
original sin that theology advanced to account for it. And
he cannot have known that his poetry effected that reconciliation between art and morality which must be
constantly renewed, or that such reconciliation was
within the power only of artists like himself with
philosophical penetration to match their literary genius.
And while he may have correctly measured his capability
against that of his immediate predecessors and contemporaries, he cannot have realized that by his sole creation he
brought English poetry into Europe and ultimately the
world.

He may not even have been sure of the intrinsic value
of what he wrote, in the face of day-to-day morality.
*Demonium cibus est carmina poetarum, secularis sapi-
encie vanitas, rhetoricum pompa verborum.* 'Demons
feed on the songs of poets, the vanity of worldly wisdom,
the pomp of rhetorical language,' reads a standard text of
his time called *The Model for a Christian.* Late in life,
possibly lowered by depression or illness, he ended his
Parson's Tale with a prayer in prose asking forgiveness
for his 'enditynges of worldly vanitees' (frivolous com-
positions). *Troilus* is the first he names, but then come
the *Duchess,* and *The House of Fame,* and the *Parlement,*

and the *Tales* of Canterbury, 'thilke that sownen into synne' (those particular ones which tend to sinfulness), and 'many another book, if they were in my remembraunce'; then, with unconscious poignancy, he falls into a line of the verse he gave to English, 'and many a song, and many a leccherous lay' (265). The works he named, which we have found essentially moral, were dangerous for the spiritually or intellectually undeveloped reader in their external worldliness. The magnificently represented beauty of the false good, or the obscenity in the low comedy, or even, simply, their sheer literary excellence, might well conceal their essential morality. This was buried too deep; they were artistically too advanced.

In the first part of his career Chaucer learned his strength, the capabilities of his language, and how to apply the one to realize the other. In the second part he applied that learning to fulfilling in himself the idea of a poet conceived by men themselves too small to attain it. His magnificent success is ironically tempered by the circumstance that there was no place for it yet in his world.

Further reading

Chaucer's works

Chaucer's English looks at first sight much like our modern language, but it is not always easy to make sense of. In the almost six centuries between us, some of the words he used have fallen out of the language; some have acquired altogether new meanings; some have confusingly extended and multiplied, or else reduced their meanings. And because so much of Chaucer's poetry is dramatic and conversational it is full of colloquial grammar and of idioms, not many of which we use today. Translation invariably fails to reproduce anything like the tones of Chaucer's language, principally because those words he used which we still use have often very different resonances. So the best way to read Chaucer, short of actually learning Middle English, is in an edition with reliable marginal or foot glosses. The outstanding edition of that kind is E. T. Donaldson's *Chaucer's Poetry: An Anthology for the Modern Reader* (New York, 1958 and reissues), which in fact contains almost all the poetry. There are editions, with marginal glosses and notes, of *Troilus and Criseyde* by John Warrington (London, 1953), and of *The Canterbury Tales* by A. C. Cawley (London, 1958). The standard edition, which has been used for the quotations in this book, is F. N. Robinson, *The Works of Geoffrey Chaucer* (2nd edn., Oxford University Press, 1957). This is best used with Norman Davis, *et al.*, *A Chaucer Glossary* (Oxford University Press, 1979). A third edition of Robinson's

Works is in preparation which will apparently have marginal glosses.

Criticism

The bulk of Chaucer criticism and interpretation is huge and its quality uneven. There is a good classified selection of titles in the Chaucer volume of the *Golden-tree Bibliographies* series, by A. C. Baugh (2nd edn., Arlington Heights, Ill., 1977). The most convenient descriptive guide to Chaucer scholarship and criticism is Beryl Rowland, *Companion to Chaucer Studies* (rev. edn., Oxford University Press: New York, 1979). Two collections of critical opinions of Chaucer over the centuries are John Burrow, *Geoffrey Chaucer: A Critical Anthology* (London, 1969), and Derek Brewer, *Chaucer: The Critical Heritage* (2 vols., London, 1978).

Chaucer's reading and sources

The independent-minded reader may find information about these the most immediately rewarding way to understanding Chaucer's achievement. There are several handy compilations of translations with commentary, and with almost no duplication: W. F. Bryan and Germaine Dempster, *Sources and Analogues of Chaucer's Canterbury Tales* (2nd edn., London, 1958); N. R. Havely, ed., *Chaucer's Boccaccio: Sources of Troilus and the Knight's and Franklin's Tales* (Cambridge University Press, 1980); Robert P. Miller, *Chaucer: Sources and Backgrounds* (Oxford University Press: New York, 1977); B. A. Windeatt, *Chaucer's Dream Poetry: Sources and Analogues* (Cambridge University Press, 1982). For understanding the behaviour-patterns of the Canterbury pilgrims the best reading is Jill Mann, *Chaucer and*

Medieval Estates Satire (Cambridge University Press, 1973).

Biography

Almost every edition of Chaucer is introduced by a 'Life', and most of these are derived from that in Robinson, which represents the best scholarship of the 1930s. Again the determined reader will want to go to the sources, and these are presented in Martin M. Crow and Clair C. Olson, eds., *Chaucer Life Records* (Oxford: Clarendon Press, 1966).

Historical and social background

The authoritative historical work on the fourteenth century is still May McKisack, The Oxford History of England series, vol. V, *The Fourteenth Century: 1307– 1399* (Oxford: Clarendon Press, 1963). For the four-teenth-century setting and cultural backgrounds the following are useful: R. S. Loomis, *A Mirror of Chaucer's World* (Princeton, NJ, 1965); Edith Rickert, *Chaucer's World*, ed. C. C. Olson and M. M. Crow (repr. New York, 1962); and D. W. Robertson, *Chaucer's London* (New York, 1968).

Index

Alain de Lille, 51, 56, 59–60
allegory, 28
Anglo-Norman literature, 23
Anne, Queen, 70
Aquinas, Thomas, 1
Aristotelianism, 1, 43–4, 51, 63
Augustine, 48, 62, 63

Blanche, Duchess of Lancaster, 22, 25, 28, 70, 71
Boccaccio, Giovanni, 32, 42–3, 47–9, 61, 91; and *Troilus and Criseyde*, 72–4, 88
Boethius, *Consolation of Philosophy*, 44, 51, 55, 63–4, 65, 74, 84, 102
Book of the Duchess, The, 22–31, 37, 67, 115
Brembre, Nicholas, 15, 17, 64
Burley, Walter, 42, 50–1

Cambridge, 11–12
Canterbury Tales, The, 56, 93–113, 114
Champaigne, Cecily, 68
Chaucer, Geoffrey: achievement, 1–3, 40, 115–16; allusions, 49; audience, 38–9; career in royal service, 3, 10, 11–21, 52–3, 64; dates of his works, 55–6; death, 21; depression, 114; dual life, 52–4; education, 10; family background, 8–10; knowledge of the world, 45–6;

marriage, 67–8; mathematical knowledge, 52; metre, 61; personality, 37, 39, 52–3; poetic identity, 37–41; reading, 42, 49–50; travel abroad, 5, 12; his understanding, 89, 91; wealth, 19–21; women and, 67–70
Chaucer, Philippa, 69–70
Christianity: alternatives to, 92–3; dogma, 90, 91–3, 105–6; human behaviour and, 101–3; and *Troilus and Criseyde*, 85, 87; war and, 104–5
Cicero, 28, 48, 51, 62, 110
Clerk's Tale, The, 46, 111
comedy, 40, 90, 95
constitutive luck, 113

Dante, 36, 37, 44, 45, 61, 87; *Divine Comedy*, 1, 32–3, 35–6, 40, 42–3, 91
Deschamps, Eustace, 31, 90
dream-vision genre, 28, 40, 56, 94

Edward III, King, 11, 12
England, medieval, 4–9; foreign wars, 6–7, 103–4
English language, 2, 26, 90
epistemology, 44, 102
eschatology, 91–3
estates satire, 54, 93, 99, 102, 103
Eve, 65